The Tuesday Afternoon]   ee

Laurie Taylor

Trentham Books

First published 1989 by
Trentham Books Limited
151 Etruria Road
Stoke-on-Trent
Staffordshire ST1 5NS
England

ISBN 0 948080 36 1

British Library Cataloguing in Publication Data
Taylor, Laurie
    The Tuesday afternoon time immemorial committee.
    1. Great Britain. Higher education
    I. Title
    378.41

    ISBN 0-948080-36-1

Acknowledgements

I would like to thank Peter Scott of the *Times Higher Education Supplement* for permission to publish this selection of pieces and for all his generous support over the past eleven years. Thanks also to my York colleagues Andy Tudor and Phil Stanworth, and my son, Matthew, for their many ideas; Claire Holland for her meticulous research; Victor Lewis-Smith for his Monday Fax machine; Cathie Mahoney for her laughter; Berrick Saul for his forbearance; Ralph Steadman for the persistently anarchic influence of his portrait; and the dozens of academics who sent me, often under plain cover, photocopied proof of the diverse forms of madness which have swept over our institutions of higher education since I began these columns back in 1978.

Contents

CHAPTER THREE
Student Matters

CHAPTER FOUR
Stresses and Strains

CHAPTER FIVE
Vice-Chancellors and Chief Executives

CHAPTER SIX
Marketing the New University

Introduction

In general, it can be said, with some confidence, that there has been no shortage of books on education, or for that matter, on higher education, in the last few years. Some of these texts have been of a very high standard, others somewhat less so, and a few, have, undoubtedly, fallen somewhere in between these two extremes.

Professor Taylor's new contribution to the field is divided into six chapters of varying lengths, with each chapter dealing with a different aspect of higher education. This seems a relatively satisfactory, if rather traditional approach, but it inevitably means that there is some material in some chapters which could possibly have gone into another chapter almost as easily as the one it is in. (It seems relevant in this context, for example, to wonder why some chapters here are so much shorter than others).

Although this is a fairly short book compared to some others, it would have been helpful if Professor Taylor had provided summaries of his main points at the beginning of each chapter, rather than leaving the reader the task of extracting information from the actual text.

Overall then, this is a valuable contribution to the field which can be recommended with some confidence to those with a specific interest in the general field. But why oh why is there no index, and why oh why, in a volume which sets out to be a comprehensive review of the literature is there no apparent reference in these pages to recent events in Iran or the precise nature of the relationship between William and Dorothy Wordsworth?

Doctor Piercemüller

Siena
Lucca
Florence

1

Departmental Developments

This is, as the last five or six Conservative Ministers with Special Responsibility for Higher Education have emphasized, a decade in which universities and polytechnics must radically depart from their traditional ideas about teaching, research and administration. There is every sign that the departments within our institutions of higher education are ready for such changes — and welcome them.

Courses are already being up-dated

THE DEPARTMENT OF CULTURAL AND MEDIA STUDIES
is proud to present its
SPRINGTIME STUDIES

Yes, why not bounce into 1989 with an exciting new course in one of the leading departments of Cultural Studies in this country. We were ranked joint 12th in last year's *THES* peer review and the most recent UGC subcommittee visit described us as "more or less on the right lines", a degree of confidence shared by our very own vice-chancellor who only this month, during a Senate debate on viability, referred to the department as "interestingly small".

Your Choice of Lecture Courses (*nb* all courses listed below have satisfied the UFC's stringent new "relevance" criterion)
● **Forward to the Channel Tunnel**
Tutor: Professor G. Lapping
Eight well-prepared, fact-laden, opinion-free lectures on this highly relevant cultural advance.

Place: Genetic Engineering Lecture Theatre
Price (for all eight lectures): Front Stalls £80; Rear Stalls £40; Restricted Vision (behind slide projector) £16.
"Yeah, on the whole I suppose it was, you know, all right" — **Mark Bostock, 2nd Year student.**
(Professor Lapping has recently appeared on *Kilroy* on BBC1)

● **Let's Have Privately Financed Motorways Running Alongside the Other Sort**
Tutor: Doctor D. Quintock
A two-term (16 lectures) course. Doctor Quintock's ability to integrate this new relevant course with the time-worn irrelevant one which he used to give on Saussurean Linguistics was recently described as 'a classic example of how to weave Chilver threads among the old".
Place: Spiller Dog Food Research Annexe
Price: £25 for 16 lectures
(Doctor Quintock is prepared to answer questions at the end of each lecture. Short factual questions, 50p; Long theoretical ones, £2.50).

● **What's Wrong with the Idea of Slashing Child Benefits.**
Tutor: Doctor Piercemüller
Doctor Piercemüller has recently returned from eight or nine long trips abroad and is therefore uniquely placed to bring a cross-cultural perspective to bear upon this highly relevant cultural issue. His one-term course commences very late in January, stops for a fortnight at the end of February, starts up for a couple of weeks in March and then grinds to a halt without warning early in April.
Place: Xerox Room (subject to availability).
Price: Admission free. (Silver collection).
"I can't speak for anyone else but I'd certainly be very pleased indeed to see Doctor Piercemüller". **Maureen (Departmental Secretary).**

Late Arrival: Please note that students arriving late for lectures will not normally be admitted until after the first concept has been fully introduced.

Publications modernized

Now, Professor Lapping, where were we? Ah yes. First of all, thank you for getting the book in on time. We've all been a bit pushed here but our messenger boy had a glance through it last Thursday and said it was "quite good", so that looks like green for go. One slight problem, though. *Title.* Yes, we all liked your suggestion of "New Directions in Cultural Studies", but I'm afraid the old computer tells us that Routledge have that title due out next month. And, unfortunately, your second choice, "New

Developments", more or less belongs to the Macmillan series, and I'm afraid that Blackwell have something of a stranglehold on "New Concepts" and "New Trends". . . Yes, we've checked out "At the Crossroads" but that's been well used recently by Pergamon, and, of course, "In Crisis", is something of a Faber copyright. . .

No, no, all's not lost. In fact we had a bit of luck only this morning. Remember a man called Grint from Monash? Works in your area? That's right. Ken Grint. "A General Theory of Cultural Studies". Well, we've heard in the last couple of hours that Doctor Grint dropped dead in our foyer this morning while delivering his next synopsis, which means, quite simply, that we are now in a position to offer you first refusal on "New Thrusts". . Jolly good. So that's "New Thrusts in Cultural Studies". *I like it.*

Now, a couple of other details while you're there. We've been playing around with figures for an hour or so in the office and we've all more or less agreed that 27 is about right. . . No, not the price, Professor Lapping. *The number of copies.* That's right. Twenty-seven copies at £85 each, which nicely allows one for every other university library, one for you (or, of course, as some of our authors prefer, your mother) and one for *The British Journal of Cultural Studies.*

One other teeny problem. The computer check we ran did also show that your own name — Lapping, that is — has already been used by two other authors in your general area this year — chap from Strathclyde and a lady from Lampeter — so we've gone straight for the nearest alphabetical alternative. And I must say it works out jolly well. In fact, I can see it now on the library shelves. "New Thrusts in Cultural Studies" by Gordon Napping.

One last bijou snagette. The photograph you sent us for the jacket. Absolutely fabulous. Very distinguished indeed. We particularly liked the relaxed pose and the way the fingers were lightly touching the point of the chin. But, we were wondering, would it take you an awfully long time to grow a smallish moustache. You see it's just that. . .

The Mass Media Cultivated

Professor Lapping — telephone. Shall I put it through?

Certainly not, Maureen. Can't you see I'm completely snowed under with this UGC questionaire?

But I thought you'd finished it on Friday?

That was *last* month's UGC questionnaire, Maureen. This is *this* month's.

I see. Well, I'll tell them you're busy. It's only Granada Television.

Hello. Professor Lapping speaking. How can I help you?

Oh, good morning, Professor Lapping. My name is Giles Pattiner. **What's New.**

Nothing much, Giles. We're still jogging along in much the same old way.

No, you misunderstand me, Professor Lapping. That's the name of the programme on which I'm the researcher. What's New. You know, "the programme which puts the week's news in context". Let me come straight to the point. This Friday we're planning to have a special edition called "May Days on the Campus in 1968".

What a truly excellent idea.

What we're going to do is dig out all the bits of old film footage, loosely string them together with some sort of commentary, and then come back to the studio to hear the views of half-a-dozen middle-aged experts.

Most innovative.

Now, Professor Lapping, were you at all involved in the events of May '68?

Quite frankly, I was up to my neck in them. Those were the heady days which earned me the sobriquet — 'Red Gordon'.

Really?

Oh yes, I remember it well: sitting around all night rapping about Jerry Rubin, Bobby Seale, Dany Cohn-Bendit and Abbie Hoffman; taking tokes on the black Afghan; dropping the odd tab of acid; digging the latest tracks from Zappa; and yet still finding the time to organize the daily 'demo'.

Really?

Oh yes. Of course we were in too much of a hurry, but we did, for those glorious few weeks in May, have a sense of being, how can I put it, yes, part of a non-material ideal, one which, of course, contrasts so vividly with today's pragmatic entrepreneurial culture.

That's excellent, Professor Lapping. Just what we want. We can offer a fee of £150, and if that's satisfactory, we look forward to seeing you on Friday in Manchester, 7 for 7.30.

Thanks so much, Giles. Only too pleased to help. Till Friday. *Ciao.* **The phone's free now, Maureen.**

Professor Lapping. Were you really that far out in May '68?

Somewhat further out in fact, Maureen. During the entire month I was on an Outward Bound course in the Trossachs. But as we now say in the Department of Cultural Studies: Never Look a Gift Horse in the Thingy.

Right on, Professor Lapping

Financial Accountability Embraced

'University Departmental Heads to be Responsible for Budget Management' — *THES* June 26.

Maureen! Come quickly!

I'm watering the plants, Professor Lapping. The geranium's wilting.

More important things, Maureen. More important things. Seven eights?

What?

Seven eights? Are they 56 or 63?

56. Seven *nines* are 63.

You're sure?

God's honour. Cross my heart and hope to die.

Excellent.

Professor Lapping. I appreciate that you're giving up valuable research time to come in during the vacation but what exactly is the point of the department having a calculator if you insist on checking each result by hand? I ask for information.

Can't take any chances, Maureen. Particularly after all those complaints we've been having about British social scientists not being numerate.

But why should calculators be wrong?

Not altogether trustworthy. Never have been. A flat battery and they start leaving figures out. Remember what happened over at Cardiff. All that nastiness. Wouldn't be surprised if they relied on calculators. Now just remind me. How does one work out what the percentage increase is from 49 to 56?

Take the smaller figure from the larger then put the result over the larger and multiply by 100 over 1.

So, 49 from 56?

Seven.

Let's get it on paper, Maureen. Remember the old rule. *Always show your workings.* You never know, we might have that chap Jarratt snooping round wanting to have a look at them some day. So that's 49 from 56. 9 from 6 won't go. So borrow 10. That's 9 from 16 leaves 7. Pay back your 10. 5 from 5 is 0. Answer 7.

Eureka!

Now that's 7 over 56 multiplied by 100 over 1. No noughts to cancel out, so it's 7 by 100. Simply move the noughts over. That gives you 700 divided by 56. 56 into 70 goes once. Put that 1 on top. Now 56 from 70 leaves 14. Bring down your 0. 56 into 140 goes twice and 28 left over. Put up your decimal point. Bring down another 0. 56 into 280.

Five.

Don't rush me, Maureen. But let's try 5, shall we? 56 by 5. 280 exactly no remainder. Excellent. The answer is 12.5. An increase in departmental expenditure on conferences abroad of over twelve per cent.

Or seven quid.

Could you just give it a final check over. Then I can move straight on to the carbon paper figures.

It's spot on, Professor Lapping.

What a relief. Great minds think alike, eh Maureen?

Professor Lapping! You old flatterer, you!

Departments Transformed into Cost Centres Overnight

Department of Cultural and Media Studies
Cost Centre Annual Report Academic Year 1987-88

EXPENDITURE

1. Room Rental
(Under the provisions of the Cost Centre agreement [1987] the university now charges £100 per week for each of the staff offices located in our department. I am delighted to say that by the simple expedient of "quadrupling up" we have been able to accommodate the entire department within two rooms thereby affecting major savings and simultaneously allowing the four members of staff seated at each of the two available desks to become substantially better acquainted with each other's ongoing research activities.)

Total Cost £5,400

2. Telephone Calls
(I am pleased to report that once again all business calls were successfully restricted to off-peak hours and lasted an average of only 1.22 minutes each. A total of four personal calls were made throughout the year. Three of these were concerned with the death or serious illness of near relatives and the remaining one was an agreed departmental call made by Doctor Quintock to see whether or not Gooch was out.)

Total cost £104.50

3. Film Hire (for History of Cinema Course)
Citizen Kane   £25

4. Typing and Duplicating Hire Charges
One Typewriter (Maureen's)   £25
One-sixth of duplicator (shared with students' union, catering, Saga Campus Holidays, psychology, and astro-physics)   £15

5. Full-time staff (including Dr Piercemüller)   £75,000
part-time   £10,000
Maureen   £6,000

Total £91,300

INCOME

1. Domestic and EEC undergraduates
(A complimentary Filofax and a one-year subscription to *Viz* for all those entering our second year course appears to have staunched the traditional outflow of first-year students.

Total Income [calculated on per capita basis for each FTE]   £71,000

2. Overseas Students
Half a Zambian postgraduate   £450

3. Conferences
"Deconstructing the concept of "genre""
"Sex, violence and lust in the contemporary cinema"   £2,800.50

4. Miscellaneous
Pick Up Grant   £25
Pump Priming Grants   £8.50
Anonymous Gift on Open Day   £0.50

5. Research Income
"An evaluation of the positive effects of heavy smoking upon student performance" (Associated Tobacco Company, Dr Quintock)
Support Expenses   £45.50

Your Board (Professor G. Lapping) is therefore able to report an overall deficit for 1987-88 of £22,538.25 (which by a coincidence is exactly my annual salary). With at least two overseas research students "fairly interested" in next year's MA course and the possibility of acquiring the department of philosophy in the near future (four staff, 114 students, two rooms and large rubber plant) your Board feels able to look to the future of this Cost Centre in a mood of quiet desperation.

Expenditure Rigidly Controlled

Case number four. Dr Ravetz, you fully understand why you have been asked to appear before this academic disciplinary committee?
Yes sir.
Good. I call upon the bursar to open the case for the prosecution.
Thank you, vice chancellor. Now, Dr Ravetz, the charge against you is that you flagrantly breached university statutes on March 30 at 11.30 am by knowingly making a long-distance personal call to a Miss Angela Shearcombe. We will hear in evidence that this call lasted for 3 minutes and 22 seconds. I repeat, THREE MINUTES AND TWENTY TWO SECONDS. Now, Dr Ravetz, do you admit the personal nature of this call?
No. Not at all. I absolutely deny it. Miss Shearcombe is a research fellow with a high standing in her profession and I wished to consult her on a matter directly relating to my current psycholinguistic research.
I see, Dr Ravetz. Will you please open the transcript of your telephone conversation which is in front of you and turn to Page One. Do you deny that your opening phrase was, "And how are you feeling today?"
That is a perfectly ordinary conversational opening.
"Feeling", "feeling", Dr Ravetz. Is that an ORDINARY word?

9

In the context, yes.

Let us turn then to Page Six, where after a long passage on what seems to be some theory or other proposed by a man with the unlikely name of Basil Bernstein, we find the following: "Is there any chance of us doing something more on this?" "Us", Dr Ravetz. "Doing something more". I put it to you. What could be more personal than that?

I. . .I. . . was only referring to the possibility of future research. That was the . . .er . . .er . . . "something more".

Really? Research? I shall have to ask the court to decide for itself whether that is the conventional meaning of the phrase "doing something more". But now, Dr Ravetz, let us leave aside these contentious matters and turn to Page 14 of the transcript — the very end of your call. Perhaps you'll be good enough to read your actual words to the court.

Yes. Yes. Erm. . . "Well, Angela. I'd better be off now. Work to do" . . .erm. . .

GO ON, Dr Ravetz, GO ON.

Erm. . . . . . "Work to do. Keep your sunny side up. Bye".

KEEP YOUR SUNNY SIDE UP. Vice Chancellor, does the court need to hear more?

I think not, bursar. The verdict is clear. Dr Ravetz, you have been found guilty of making a blatantly personal *and* long distance call before one o'clock. Only one sentence is possible. You will be taken from this court to a place of execution behind the sports complex and there hung by the neck. Now, number five on your list. Professor Fuller and the case of the disappearing internal memo pad. Your witness, bursar.

Even at Christmas

Right. Starred Business. Thank you, student reps — And, Maureen, if you wouldn't mind leaving us as well. The next item is purely staff business. Do you mind?

Certainly not, Professor Lapping. I'll go and arrange next year's timetable, send round a reminder note about supervisors' reports, talk to six or seven students about their personal problems, organize the Christmas party, and finish typing Mr Odgers' PhD dissertation.

Excellent. Now, if the rest of us could turn to item 1 under Starred Business: *Christmas Arrangements.* I believe you wish to speak to this, Doctor Quintock.

Yes indeed. I'm afraid I have to raise a very serious issue relating to the organization of the annual Christmas collection for cleaners and secretaries. I see from the letter I received last Tuesday that this year professors are being asked to contribute £3 each, senior lecturers £2, and lecturers £1.50.

Surely a very equitable scheme, Doctor Quintock.

As far as it goes, Professor Lapping. As far as it goes. But in the middle of this scale is a gross anomaly. Whereas professors are asked for £3, and senior lecturers for £2, readers like myself, who enjoy no financial advantages whatsoever over senior lecturers, are asked to donate £2.50.

I'm afraid the proposal is a purely practical one, Doctor Quintock. You see, without that additional 50p from your good self it is simply not possible to afford our traditional two one-pound boxes of chocolates for the cleaners or the equally traditionally two-pound Presentation Box for Maureen.

Might not this awkward problem be solved by purchasing somewhat less expensive chocolates?

Thank you, Doctor Piercemüller. But as you might recall, had you been present at last year's meeting on this topic, this was a strategy adopted at that time in order to make up for the loss in contributions occasioned by the non-replacement of teaching staff. The cleaners were moved down from *All Gold* to their present *Moonlight,* and *Dairy Box* was substituted for Maureen's traditional *Black Magic.*

But might it not still be possible to purchase something a little less expensive, than, say, *Moonlight*?

I'm no expert in this area, Doctor Bugle, but I believe that *Moonlight* is — how could one put this — a fairly basic box of chocolates , and that if one moves further down the scale then one reaches those products which fall outside the normally agreed definition of a "box of chocolates". I'm thinking here, of course, of Cadbury's *Roses* and *Quality Street.*

Professor Lapping, I must say that I do sympathise with Doctor Quintock over this. Perhaps, our only way out of this dilemma lies along the path of frankness. What we should do, I believe, is to continue in our traditional manner. That is, hand over the Presentation Dairy Box *to Maureen. . .*

Doctor Tench?

And then ask, in as Christmassy way as possible, if she would be so good as to contribute 50p towards the cost.

New Departmental Duties Allocated

Dear Departmental Colleague

I am writing in my capacity as Chairperson of the Internal Appointments Committee to indicate that the following departmental administrative positions will shortly become vacant.

1. Undergraduate Library Placator

Basic Duties: Pointing out to anxious and hysterical students who can't find a single one of their essential course books in the library that there is a jolly sight more to university than sitting about reading.

Hours: Approximately 15 per week

2. Mature Student Recruiting Officer

Basic Duties: Standing on an upturned packing case in City Square extolling the virtues of the Department of Cultural and Media Studies to anyone over 21 who looks as though they might be remotely interested in a little higher education.

Hours: By arrangement with a man who sells books by Ron Hubbard and two slightly aggressive youths from the Revolutionary Workers Party.

3. Special Envoy to the Vice Chancellor

Basic Duties: Nodding affectionately and smiling eagerly in the general direction of the Vice Chancellor at every available opportunity.

Hours: approximately 12 per week (entertaining allowance of £15).

4. UGC Questionnaire Respondent

Basic Duties: Filing in UGC questionnaires and/or university or faculty or departmental questionnaires prompted by UGC questionnaires.

Hours: Approximately 72 per week.

5. Departmental Photocopier Monitor

Basic Duties: Peering through a small hole in the ceiling of the photocopying room and noting down the names of colleagues who fail to enter the correct number of copies taken in the Photocopier Book.

Hours: 12 per week (randomly distributed).

6. Overseas Student Acceptance Officer

Basic Duties: Offering immediate and unconditional acceptance to any overseas graduate student with money regardless of their total lack of appropriate qualifications and the subsequent need to persuade the external examiner that they should be given the benefit of the doubt because of "language difficulties".

Hours: 20 minutes per term. (approximately 10 interviews).

These are all, in their various ways, thoroughly rewarding tasks, and I'm only sorry that I will have to give them up during my forthcoming sabbatical term. I look forward to receiving your nominations.

Yours

Gordon Lapping (Head of Department and Honorary Health and Safety Officer)

The Material Infrastructure Monitored

"Our crumbling universities". (Headline in The THES)

Now, shall we take Item Seven — *Timetable for the Spring Term* — before the smoking break?

Do we really need a smoking break, Professor Lapping? I thought it had been established that no one in the Department now smoked.

That's correct, Doctor Hakemaster, but we did agree by a narrow majority that the smoking break should be retained because it provided Doctor Rayburn with an opportunity to exercise her German Sheepdog.

I'm sorry, I'd forgotten.

That's perfectly all right. Item Seven, then? Yes, Doctor Wernitz, if you'd like to lead us through this one.

Of course, sir, I think everything is now pretty straightforward. Mr Odgers, as last term, will take sole responsibility for *Radical Perspectives in Media Studies* and *Buckets in "A" Corridor*. Professor Teetlebaum will continue with second year *Semiotics and Saussure* and *B Block Mops*.

Does that still include *Brooms,* Doctor Wernitz?

Yes indeed, Professor Teetlebaum, but only in the case of Everyday Seepage. When conditions call for *Advanced Bailing* then, of course you will have your usual assistance from Doctor Gresham of Abnormal Psychology.

Thank you.

Then, Doctor Piercemüller. Is he here at the moment?

Unfortunately not, Doctor Wernitz. Apparently he's rather tied up at home — something about it already being past the twelfth day and the decorations not being down.

I see. Well, perhaps someone could note that his course on *Linguistic Relativism* commences this term, and that his other departmental responsibility will be for *Sudden Gaps in the Floor*.

I wonder if we might deal with my timetable at this point, Doctor Wernitz. Auslander seems to be getting a little frisky.

Certainly, Doctor Rayburn. Your major responsibility will be for *Advanced Socio-Linguistics* and *Clearing Fallen Concrete Chunks From Around The Outside of the Building*. And as before, we'd be only too happy if in the case of larger chunks you felt able to call upon help from Auslander.

Thank you, Doctor Wernitz.

Finally, I myself will continue with *Transformational Grammar and Precarious Blackboards,* Doctor Comstock will handle *Elaborated and Restricted Codes* and *Trapped Lifts,* and Professor Lapping who is on sabbatical has kindly agreed to carry on with *Postgraduate Hermeneutics* and *Badly Jammed Doors*. And one piece of good news. The problem over the lavatories in B Block has now eased and the Bursar will be returning to his usual office thus making the small camping site in Car Park D available for

13

the student counsellor. Any questions?
It seems not, Doctor Wernitz.
Then, may I propose we accept this term's timetable?
Woof! Woof!
Thank you, Auslander. Time for walkies, everyone.

New Responsibilities Embraced

'The existence of a class of administrative "servants" has increased the ability of the academic staff to retreat from responsibility.' (Geoffrey Lockwood, Registrar, Sussex University, *THES,* April 11).

Ah Maureen. There you are. Busy?
Not really, Professor Lapping. Not really. Just got to finalize this term's timetable, check the examination papers, collate last term's tutorial forms, send out invitations to the Departmental Open Day, and water Dr Piercemüller's plants. Otherwise I'm pretty clear all morning.
Excellent. Look, d'you think you could give someone in the Adminstration a ring and tell them that I went into Lecture Hall B6 this morning to give the first lecture of term and found the blackboard *covered* in chalk from the previous lecture. Numbers, symbols, graphs. God knows what else.
Chalk? On the board?
That's right, Maureen.
Gosh, Professor Lapping. Erm. . . who should I ring in Administration? Registrar's department or Bursar's?
I think it sounds more like Registrar's than Bursar's. Yes, Registrar's. The Bursar mostly does money. The Registrar handles, you know, more, well, general matters.
Ah. Anyone in particular in the Registrar's department?
D'you know, I've rather lost touch recently. Who's there now? Is old Sheridan still around?
He, died, Professor Lapping. Two or three years ago.
Oh I'm sorry. You knew him did you?
No. But I remember the collection.
Great pity. Excellent chap. Well, who's there now? Who's on the list?
There's the Deputy Registrar, Mr Sloanes. Quite pleasant on the phone. Slight stutter. Or the Assistant Registrar, Mr Gretton. And two Senior Administrative Officers Ms Kettleby and Mr Wilcox.
Good heavens! What a collection! Deputies. Assistants. Senior Administrative Assistants. And no doubt Assistant Senior Administrative Assistants. Eh? And here I am as Head of Department running the whole caboodle virtually single-handed. Makes you think, doesn't it Maureen?

It certainly does, Professor Lapping.
I'll tell you what, Maureen. I bet you there's just as many deputies and assistants in the Bursar's department. I mean, what on earth can these people be doing all day? I mean, how *do* they fill their time?
I'm not certain of the exact details, Professor Lapping, but I expect. . .
Expect what, Maureen?
Well, I expect quite a few of them have their work cut out going round cleaning all the blackboards.

Secretaries Are On Their Toes

April 30th
STUDENT REPORTS
Please would you make sure that all reports on third-year students are submitted to the office by the end of next week (May 8th) so that these may be collated in time for the Examiners Meeting.
Thanks.

May 8th
STUDENT REPORTS
Sorry to have to bother you again, but we are still waiting for some third-year student reports. Remember, these are now urgently needed for collation in readiness for the Examiners Meeting.
By Monday please.

May 14th
STUDENT REPORTS
Final note. Any outstanding student reports must be submitted by tomorrow (May 15th) if they are to be available at the Examiners Meeting.

May 21st
STUDENTS REPORTS
Maureen tells me that one or two members of the department have still not submitted reports on their third-year students. I know that this is a particularly busy part of the term but please note that Maureen needs these reports *by return* if she is to complete her collation in time for the Examiners Meeting.

May 28th
STUDENTS REPORTS
Listen. I want to talk to you all about my notes. That's right. My notes. I mean on April 30th (Yes, that's right, back in April) I wrote asking you politely for student reports and giving you a whole week to send them in

15

What happened? *Nothing.* Not one report. *Silence.*

So I tried again. Right? Tried another track. On May 8th it was "Sorry to bother you again". Bother? Yes, that's what I wrote. *Sorry to bother you with a request so basic that in any other area of normal academic life it might have been regarded as totally unnecessary. Again nothing happened. Not a damn thing.*

Then May 14th. Yes? Remember? a *third* note. I used a little psychology there, didn't I? I wrote "any outstanding reports". Right? Tried to isolate you a little. *Were you the only one?* That sort of thing. But, you know what? EVERY ONE OF YOU KNEW THAT I'D NOT RECEIVED A SINGLE REPORT. Didn't you?

And then my *final* ploy. Yes, a *fourth* note. May 21st. "Maureen tells me . . ." "Maureen needs". It's not me any longer, you see. It's *Maureen.* Your poor departmental secretary, who works twice as hard as any of you for exactly one quarter of the money, can't begin to do her job because of your crass inefficiency. Right?

And I'll tell you all something. Do you know I STILL HAVEN'T RE-CEIVED A SINGLE REPORT. NOT ONE. What's the matter with my notes? Not to your taste perhaps. You don't like the grammar? Or the style? Would you like me to send a little money with each request. *Some blood perhaps?*

Now listen very carefully. This is my last note, my final request, a deadline beyond whose bourne no traveller returns, my ultimate plea. This is the note about the note about the note about the note about the note.

But it's not reports I want this time. No, something far simpler. I want a *sign.* Anything will do. A mere mark on the paper, an X, some spilt tea. Anything. But I must know. IS THERE ANYBODY OUT THERE?

Their Value Appreciated

Morning, Professor Lapping.

Good Morning, Maureen. My word it's a chilly one.

Can you spare a second?

Of course, Maureen. What seems to be the trouble?

Well, I'm sorry to bother you, sir, but did you notice anything different about the office this morning?

Well, it certainly looks very tidy. Very tidy indeed. Nice and neat.

No, not that.

Erm. . . ah yes of course. There on the board. You've completed next term's undergraduate timetable. Jolly good. All smartly drawn up.

No, not quite that.

Well. . . let me see. . . yes, you've also, as usual, allocated all the teaching rooms for the lectures and seminars, making certain that Dr Wernitz has

his normal one with the extra large blackboard and that Dr Sprague is in B313 where the central heating system doesn't affect his sinuses.

Go on.

Oh yes. There, underneath, are the appropriate student groups for each seminar and tutorial, all efficiently designed so that joint-degree and single-subject students have their own groups, and that the well-known Marxists are kept right away from Dr Stumaker.

Anything else?

Well of course, you'll have liaised with the administration and four other departments in order to ensure that there aren't any timetable or room clashes and that we don't have a repetition of last term's farce in which Dr Wernitz's lecture on structuralism clashed in D461 with student performances of *Oi for England*.

More.

Mmmm. I suppose that you'll have followed normal procedure and properly taken into account the very understandable difficulties that staff have over accommodating their research and their teaching duties, by carefully limiting the teaching hours to the later parts of the morning and early afternoon while keeping most Mondays and Fridays clear.

Any other little things?

Just give me a second. Ah yes, I see all the filing trays are clear. So in your usual way, you've managed to bring all the student records up to date and written to members of staff reminding them that certain tutorial reports are still outstanding from the terms before last. You'll have also filed all the department's correspondence, reminded staff of forthcoming university committees, arranged a series of semi-fictional entries for the university newsletter, dealt with half a dozen telephone enquiries from parents about the admission of their children to next year's course, and probably comforted three or four students in various stages of nervous breakdown.

Almost there. Just one other teeny thing.

No. You've got me there. OK, just a minute. How silly of me. You've wearing a pretty new dress.

Not that.

No?

No.

I give up.

I'm standing on my desk with a rope around my neck!

New Technology Arrives to Help

Good. So that seems to be agreed. We'll all write as individuals to the UGC about the restructuring of the universities, except over the issue of extra car parking space for senior lecturers, where we'll express a departmental view.

Now, item six. *Results of the Survey Carried out by the Departmental Word Processor Subcommittee.* Yes. Doctor Wernitz, this, I believe, is very much your pigeon.

Yes, thank you, Professor Lapping. I presume that I hardly need to remind anyone, that this is the survey upon which it was agreed, after somewhat protracted, even heated, but always well-informed discussion, that we should base our departmental decision about the purchase of this particular piece of advanced technology. In this era of rapidly changing. . .

Do get a move on Doctor Wernitz. There are still nearly eight items of non-student business to be covered. I think we can take all that business about "moving with the times" for granted.

I'm sorry, Professor Lapping. May I then move immediately to the first part of the survey — and here, as elsewhere, may I acknowledge the methodological help we received throughout the course of our work from Doctor Comstock.

Here, here,

Now, in this first section we concentrated upon the possible benefits for staff which might lie in the correcting and display facilities of the processor.

As I remember, you specifically asked for academic articles which might be improved before publication by this means.

Exactly. Unfortunately only one article was submitted to the committee — from Doctor Piercemüller — and we were unable to see how this might benefit from the relatively modest technology we were considering.

Might we know the precise problem?

It was mainly a question of very poor grammar.

Ah.

We then turned to the issue of updating book lists — that is, the capacity of the machine for storing book lists in a manner which allows for additional alphabetically ordered entries to be made at any time. However, our findings indicate that most book lists in the department have not undergone revisions in the last ten years, and furthermore, 82 per cent of those departmental members who responded were of the opinion that "nothing worth reading" had been produced in their subject area during that period.

Pretty conclusive.

Yes indeed. Then we turned to student records, concentrating here on the machine's ability to provide detailed information on a student's academic record, background qualifications and tutorial progress during the course. But here again, there was little positive benefit perceived, with 92 per cent of the departmental memebrs ticking the statement: "I know far too much about the students already, thank you very much."

So the balance of opinion was running pretty strongly against purchase. Doctor Wernitz?

Quite so, Professor Lapping. But I'm pleased to say that the situation was quite reversed when we came to the final question. And here, as you will see from the summary in front of you, there was complete agreement.

Excellent. So may we now minute this decision. "It was agreed that we should now proceed with the purchase of a Departmental Word Processor on the grounds. . ." Could I have the exact words here. Doctor Wernitz? "On the grounds that. . ."
"That the Politics Department has got one already".
Excellent.

And Must Be Safeguarded

The Departmental Office, September 13th

Dear Professor Lapping,

Thank you very much for your postcard which I've now put up on the Departmental noticeboard. (Do all the women in Ibiza really go round the beach like that?)

As you will know it's now getting nearer to the beginning of a new term and I'm accordingly writing to you at Dr Quintock's suggestion to bring you up to date on some "confidential matters"

You'll be pleased to hear that we've been able to retain your professorial phone-line. That is, the one with a direct outside line which can be used between three and half-past four in the afternoon. But as you'll remember the university is very concerned about this privilege being abused so special combination locks have been fitted to such phones. Your secret number, without which you'll be unable to lift the receiver, is: 84-42-78-36-19.

Unfortunately this is easily confused with the departmental confidential number for using the photocopier, a system which we were forced to introduce this year when we found that the Psychology Department (typical!) had been doing hundreds of copies without paying. The number to dial here is: 85-43-61-36-19.

Some other secrets. There is still a professional "hot-line" to the Vice Chancellor which of course is only available in cases of extreme emergency (e.g. some vague indication in a colleague of the onset of a terminal illness) but this has now been changed from 9471 to 8632, and in order to circumvent the possibility of the number being accidentally discovered by outsiders, you are asked to introduce yourself initially with your "designated nom-de-plume". The Registrar rang yesterday to tell me that the theme for this year will be *Animals of the Englôh Countryside* and your personal name will be:
BADGER
Finally, something about The-Word-Processor-and-Computer. This is a brand new piece of equipment which was bought last year by our department (in conjunction with Nalgo, the Catering Department and the Sports Centre) to help out with secretarial and administrative problems. I'm afraid that I haven't yet seen it myself because ever since it arrived Dr Quintock

19

has spent night and day sitting looking at the screen, getting what he calls "the hang of it". But he did decide last month to put all the secret staff and student files "on to it", so that we now need a secret code (available only to Dr Quintock, me, you, and someone from the Catering Department).You must first "log in" with your number which is: 8746392, and then give your password (this has to be slightly obscure because apparently some student "hackers" are very good at guessing such passwords as "wives names" etc). Your word is therefore: ZEUGMA (Dr Quintock says "just think of 'syllepsis' ").

That's all the secret things for the time being so I'll say goodbye for the moment and will of course be in touch again shortly about your timetable (yes, I have remembered about Mondays, Tuesdays, and Thursdays!)
Best Wishes
Maureen (Department Secretary)
P.S. I'm sorry this letter is in such a state but when Doctor Quintock saw it lying on my desk he immediately crumped it up and threw it into the waste-paper basket.

Computerisation Is Vital

May I now formally declare the examiners' meeting open and warmly welcome the new external examiner, our old friend and former colleague, Professor Dingbatte. Nice to have you with us, Norman.

Thank you Charles.

Now to the real business. The marks themselves. And as you all know this is a very exciting year for us all in that it is the first time in which the undergraduate degree marks have benefited from full computerization. Not an easy task. Indeed, before we turn to the first candidate, might I suggest that we minute our thanks to Dr Hatter for the many hours that he has devoted to this project over the last 12 months?

Hear, hear.

As you will see, Dr Hatter has a thingy in front of him which enables him to calculate the final marks for each candidate as we go along — and he can then read them off from the other thingy on his right. But enough of the technicalities. Can we go from the top of the list? Candidate 1376. Average mark, please, Dr Hatter.

The average mark for candidate 1376 is 56.84.

So that would be a 2.2?

Yes, but there is a lateness factor to be inputted. This, as you will remember, is calculated as .5 of a mark for each day late, and so with an overall lateness score of 24 days, we have a 12 marks deficit which I am now asking the compute to relate to the overall average — and it tells me that the mark is now 55.27.

A middling 2.2?

Yes indeed. But then there is the joint degree cross-weighting factor in which all marks for options taken in the politics department receive a .3 increment because of the smaller number of papers taken in that degree. There are two politics options for 1376 and the computer informs me that this moves the average mark up to 55.97.

More or less a solid 2.2?

That's right. Finally, there is the joint project mark of 60 which receives a double weighting compared to the marks of other examination papers, and as this was also a half politics project the usual extra politics weighting produces a final candidate mark for 1376 of 56.83.

So a 2.2?

Exactly.

And now, Dr Peewit, following our usual procedure, may we have the name of candidate 1376?

Yes indeed. Candidate 1376 is Gillian Dabsworth.

An extremely pleasant student.

Very polite girl. And most helpful.

A little shy, perhaps. But certainly a trier.

Yes, slightly hesitant. A nice sense of humour, though.

Well, thank you everybody for those comments. Most helpful and relevant. I get the general impression that we're thinking here of a 2.1 for Gillian. Good. Can we pop that news into the computer. Dr Hatter?

I've already fed in the amendment, sir, and here comes the readout.

Yes, Dr Hatter. What does it say?

It simply says: I SOMETIMES WONDER WHY I BOTHER.

Other Technology Is Not Ignored

Hello, is that the video centre?

No, I'm afraid not.

The *video* centre?

No. This is the university *audio-visual* centre.

Ah yes, of course, audio-visual centre. Well, it's Professor Lapping here. Lapping. Professor of culture and media studies.

Oh yes, professor. I don't think we've met, have we? I'm Lazenby.

Lazenby? Are you sort of. . . erm. . . on the technical side of things?

I'm *Director* of the audio-vidual centre.

Are you? Lazenby? Oh yes. Of course you are. Silly of me. Well, Lazenby. How are things these days in the . . .erm. . .erm. . . the old centre?

Not so good really. As you know we're very much in the firing line for the next round of cuts. We've already lost three technicians. And of course all this at a time when audio-visual techniques and services are more and

more fundamentally linked to advances in higher education.

Oh yes. You're right there. Lazenby. Absolutely right. An incredibly short-sighted policy. Exactly what's wrong with this country if you don't mind me saying so.

Exactly. But of course not everybody appreciates that. We have to convince all those traditional academics who can't see much further than formal lectures and written texts.

How true. Yes, you've put your finger on it there Ponsonby. The critical thing is to get the message across. I can tell you there's already a lot of sympathy for the sort of . . .erm. . . work you're doing. Oh yes.

Well, what can I do for you professor?

Ah yes. Well look here Ponsonby. I've got a sort of newish course which I may be giving in the very near future — more or less concerned with what we tend to call semiology and structuralism. But I don't want to blind you with science.

No, please.

Well I shall be wanting to draw on some sort of audio-visual presentations — say paradigmatic versions — which would enable me to more or less home in on what I might call the combinatory of features of a particular visual genre. That sort of thing. D'you see the sort of thing I'm after?

Oh yes, sir.

You do. You know the sort of thing I want?

Yes. You'd like me to videotape _Dial M for Murder_ on _BBC1_ tonight. If that's not too much trouble.

Fine.

And sort of mark it "personal" when you send it across, would you?

Right you are.

And jolly good luck in the future with your video centre.

Thank you sir.

Departmental Meetings Streamlined

If everyone's finished tea perhaps we could reconvene and move straight on to item six on the agenda: "The Jarratt Recommendations on Streamlining Committees". Yes, Doctor Quintock, you wish to speak to this item?

Not directly, Professor Lapping.

_Ah._

In fact, I wish to raise a procedural point relating to our recent tea break. I was wondering if there would be any support for a proposal that at future departmental meetings the siting of the biscuit plate could be alternated. Once again those of us at the unfavourable end of the table have found ourselves denied the option of selecting either chocolate digestives or jammy dodgers.

Thank you, Doctor Quintock. Perhaps we might content ourselves with

noting your remarks and return to the subject at a later date.
I'm sorry, Professor Lapping.
Yes, Mr Odgers?
I really don't think we can record Doctor Quintock's remark without also making it perfectly clear that at least two of the jam biscuits which were originally available for selection at this so-called "favourable" end of the table, were in fact eaten by Doctor Robards' dog.
May I come in at this point, Professor Lapping?
If you must, Doctor Turnbull.
I would like to take this opportunity to raise the whole question of the attendance at our meetings of Doctor Robards' dog.
Hear. Hear.
It is positively disconcerting to glance down during a serious discussion and realize that it has once again thrust its face into one's lap. What's more, and here I'm speaking personally and not in my capacity as Chairperson of Graduate Committee, I much resent the manner in which it continually moves around underneath the table. It is nothing short of prowling.
Hear. Hear.
Would it be helpful, Professor Lapping, if we could hear Doctor Robards' views. It is, after all, his dog.
Quite so, Doctor Campling. But as you will appreciate such views are difficult to obtain since Doctor Robards took advantage of the early retirement scheme last January.
But how does his dog get here?
I believe it walks. It is apparently inordinately fond of our gatherings. According to my information it sets off from home every other Wednesday during term, stays for the entire meeting, and returns home immediately afterwards.
I wonder if a compromise might be in order, Professor Lapping?
I would hope so, Doctor Campling.
Well, sir, it seems somewhat unreasonable to blame Doctor Robards' dog for its tendency to prowl. What is more, it clearly displays a keenness for our meetings and an overall attendance record which might be the envy of some of our senior staff. In these circumstances might it not be a sufficient sanction to exclude the dog from that portion of the meeting to which we already accord a privileged status.
Get on with it, Campling.
Might I suggest, sir, that we exclude Doctor Robards' dog from starred business?

CHAPTER TWO

The Thoroughly Modern Academic

In today's higher education there is no longer any room for old-fashioned dons selfishly pursuing the life of the mind. Today's academic is out in the real world, meeting real people, grappling with real problems.

Academics should stop cowering in the secret garden of knowledge and get to grips with the real world — Robert Jackson, undersecretary of state for higher education — THES June 17.

They can't hide from me. I'll flush them out.
Gently, Mr Jackson. You'll frighten them.
What's that noise? I heard a noise.
Shhh. Look there. By the herbaceous border.
Where? Where?
Come a little closer. Yes, just as I thought. A little gathering of the Humanities.
And are they cowering?
Oh yes. One or two are almost completely covered by a dense concern with the relation between truth and beauty.
A dose of reality would do them good.
And still others are buried deep in a controversy about the manner in which literature might express the spirit of an ideal organic community.
We'll send in some ferrets. They'll do the trick. Lead on. What else is there lurking on this campus?
Shhhh. Over there.
I can't see anything.
Get closer. By the rhododendrons.
What is it?

A tiny herd of Social Scientists.
How many?
No more than six.
And skulking?
Oh yes. One or two are almost completely concealed behind some fundamental questions about the nature of the just society.
And the others?
They're crouched under a debate about the paradoxes inherent in the promotion of an ethic of individualism in an era of corporate capitalism.
We'll put the beaters on them. Drive them out like grouse. Now lead on. What next?
Look! There under the trees in the far distance. A rare sight nowadays. Three or four grazing philosophers.
Why do they look so small?
They're bent double by their teaching loads. Look. Two of them are burrowing right down into the concept of realism itself.
We'll soon drag them into the light of day.
While another delves into the ideology which is promoted by the very notion of a real world with which one might "get to grips".
Send for the tanks. It's the only answer. Rip away every inch of this protective cover. Clear the thickets of epistemology. Uproot all ambiguities. Defoliate conceptual distinctions. Back to the real world.
But, Minister, when all that's gone, this real world will only be a wasteland.
Nonsense. Mr Ridley's bungalows arrive next Thursday.

Staff Are Engaged In Self-Appraisal

Doctor Piercemüller is here now, Professor Lapping.
Thank you, Maureen. Would you be so good as to drop whatever you're doing and join us — nothig too pressing, I hope?
Not really, no. I was just registering 45 new first years, typing up three booklists which I've just received from tutors for the new term, planning seminar rooms for the entire academic years, and watering Doctor Quintock's spider plants.
Excellent. Well, let's make a start. Yes, do come in, Doctor Piercemüller.
You wanted to see me?
Yes, indeed, Doctor Piercemüller. Do take a seat. I wanted to have a little chat with you about appraisal.
Appraisal?
That's it. As you may recall, the vice chancellor and the SAS — that's the Special Appraisal Squad — met during the long vacation and in accordance with the Secretary of State's wishes, decided to initiate university wide appraisal schemes — the first phase of which would be peer appraisals. So,

in line with this decision, I have now invited you to my office this morning for an appraisal session — a session in which I will ask you to speak openly and frankly to me about what you believe to be your particular academic strengths and weaknesses. Maureen is here to keep a record of our little meeting. Is that perfectly clear? Right. Off we go. Doctor Piercemüller, perhaps we could start with administration. I see that you are our departmental representative on the Bookshop Committee. Now, how would you rate your performance at this task. Average, Above Average, or Below Average?

No comment.

What's that?

I'm not talking to you.

Not talking?

That's right. As there is every indication that the AUT will shortly be recommending non-cooperation in all appraisal schemes, I have nothing more to say.

You won't even tell me how you think your administrative work is going?

No.

Oh, go on.

No, I won't.

Well, how about teaching? Would you say, for example, that you were completely happy or only fairly happy with your lecturing over the last year?

No comment.

And how about research. Would you rate your publication record in the last 12 months as Prolific, Average or Virtually Non-Existent?

Get lost.

You do realize that you are an extremely obstinate man, Doctor Piercemüller?

And do you realize you are an insensitive time-serving bore?

Hardly as time-serving, if I may so, as a deadbeat like yourself who has made no positive contribution to the intellectual life of this department for the past decade.

Hark who's talking! Someone whose dismal record in basic research has made him the laughing stock of the entire academic community.

Good morning, Doctor Piercemüller. You may go.

Thank you.

Maureen.

Professor Lapping?

Maureen, May I offer you my most sincere apologies for taking up your time on such a busy day with this futile exercise in peer appraisal.

Not at all, Professor Lapping. In fact, I thought it went rather well.

Even At The Top

"Self-appraisal assessment on the way for lecturers" — THES *November 21, 1986.*

Do try and relax, Professor Lapping. I'm only trying to find out what you think of yourself, of your own abilities.

I do appreciate that, Vice chancellor.

No one has been spying on you, bugging your lectures and seminars, interviewing your students. This is *self*-appraisal, Professor Lapping. Try and remember George's reasurring words.

George?

George *Walden.* The under-secretary of state for higher education. Only last week he was explaining that, although appraisal was essential, it was not, and I quote, "a new inquisition by a sadistic goverment". All right?

Yes. Thank you, Vice chancellor.

So may we proceed? *Good.* Now, how would you rate yourself as a lecturer?

Erm. . . good. Yes, good. B to B + .

Quite sure? Do be honest. It's only yourself you're cheating.

Well, not perhaps B + . Not quite as good as Doctor Quintock. He makes them laugh. He's before me in A237. Once I even heard them clapping. And he gets more students then me. Some don't come to my lectures at all. And some of those that do. . .

Go on.

. . .throw paper aeroplanes.

I respect your honesty, Professor Lapping. Very good self-appraisal. Now perhaps some of your stronger points. Seminars? Tutorials? Do you enjoy meeting students in that context?

Nobody ever speaks. I can't seem to ask questions any more. They look straight back at me as though I'd made another statement. Once, I tried keeping silent. They all stood up and left.

Professor Lapping, this is indeed an object lesson in self-appraisal. But to brighter matters. How about personal supervision? Do you find you're able to help students with their personal troubles? Is this a plus factor?

I've not had one decent problem in the last five years.

Perhaps you're simply lucky with your supervisees.

Oh no. They have abortions, try to commit suicide, change sex, transfer to other departments, but they don't tell me.

I see. Well, Professor Lapping — Gordon — you have spoken with commendable honesty, with almost ruthless self-insight, of your administrative inefficiency, your pedagogic ineptitude, and your supervisory incompetence.

All very C minus I'm afraid.

Quite so. And I'm rather left wondering — in a purely bureaucratic sense, you understand — what exactly I should pop down here as your greatest

strength. Something, that is, which you are particularly proud of yourself.
Well, it may not be strictly relevant, Vice chancellor, but. . .
Yes. Go on.
Well, peoople have said I make a rather splendid vinaigrette.

And The Very Top

Five Front Runners as Vice Chancellors Prepare to Select a New Chairman.

"Look let me get this one."
"Thanks so much."
"Large Booths?"
"Please."
"Actually, I rather wanted to have a word with you about, you know . . ."
"Ah, yes."
"I was wondering about your thoughts on Edward. Could you see him in the job?"
"Most certainly. A thoroughly sound chap. Although one does just wonder if there might not be a teeny bit of tension with, you know, thingy."
"Thingy?"
"Sir Thingy."
"Ah yes, I see what you mean. So possibly you'd rather go for David?"
"Wouldn't hear a word against him. Thoroughly sound. Although in these difficult political times, he is perhaps a shade. . .how can I put it. . . a shade, irresolute."
"I see. So does that rather bring Mark into the picture?"
"Oh yes. A very, very sound chap. One has hardly any reservations at all about Mark."
"No?"
"No. Although there are moments — I'll go no further than that — moments, when one can detect the faintest hint of complacency."
"So perhaps you'd consider John as a more serious contender?"
"Oh yes. First-rate chap. Sound as a bell. No doubt about it. A little equivocal here and there but otherwise above criticism."
"Which rather leaves Graham?"
"Must be a front runner. Very talented indeed. And one hardly notices the occasional streak of ingenuousness."
"So all in all you have minor reservations about all five front runners — about Mark, David, Edward, Graham and John."
In a sense, yes. Although, of course, they're all sound chaps."
"What sort of person would you favour yourself?"
"Someone with a mind of their own."

29

"Quite so."
"**Someone able to make public pronouncements with confidence and spirit.**"
"Splendid."
"**Someone who stands out from the crowd.**"
"Yes, yes."
"**Someone capable of rising well above the surrounding bureaucracy.**"
"Sounds ideal."
Someone with integrity and guts."
"Hallelujah."
"**Someone — this is the best job description I can think of — someone no university appointments committee in the country would ever dream of having as their vice chancellor.**"
"That's our man!"

Courses Are Made More RELEVANT

"Before we start I wonder if I might ask Professor Drunger to extinguish his cigar. Sorry to mention it Douglas, but as you will recall, we did decide last term that smoking might only take place while agenda items having even numbers were being discussed. Excellent. Right, item 1: two new proposals for academically second-rate but commercially sound postgraduate courses. Dr Tranter would you like to speak to your submission?"

"*Thank you sir, I think the document probably speaks for itself. Basically the proposal is for a new diploma, which, with appropriate reference (or should one say deference), to our sponsor, we are calling the Trust House Forte diploma in hotel management and gourmet catering. There are good signs that there is a demand for such a course in overseas countries, particularly those with a developing tourist potential. We have, for example, already received enquiries from Chad and Oman. As you see, we've initially fixed the fees at £6,000 per annum, but this does of course include a sum for the purchase of essential equipment, such things as . . .erm. . . mixers, graters, pudding bowls, drying-up cloths. That sort of thing.*"

"I think my only reservation here, Dr Tranter, is about expertise. I wonder if you can do anything to persuade us that the ideal department to handle such a course is the department of philosophy. Might it not be more appropriately located, say, in the department of social administration?"

"*I do take this point, sir, but if I might remind you of your own remarks in last year's annual report to senate. 'No department can any longer rely on its established reputation, the advent of academic monetarism means that our new operational principle must be dog eats dog.' I think our own readiness to enter the marketplace has been well established in our part time PhD programme on* Love Lives of the Great Philosophers.*"

"Spirited advocacy. Doctor Tranter. Spirited advocacy. I think after that we can only wish you and your colleagues well. Now Professor Frink, you have a second proposal to place before us, I understand."

"Exactly sir. Basically what we in the department of peace studies would like to propose is an MA(SAS): that is a two-year taught course which would enable students to consider theoretical and practical aspects of SAS work with particular reference to the relationship between SAS successes and the revival of Britain as a major world power."

"You have, I understand, taken expert advice on this course?"

"Indeed sir. We've had several very interesting and, of course confidential, discussions about the syllabus with Professor X. and we already have an impressive list of guest lecturers which includes Brigadier Y and hopefully Dr W. As we indicate in our submission, we have got over the problem of preserving anonymity in this sensitive area by allowing such experts to lecture from behind the blackboard."

"Most promising. Just one small point: I appreciate the need to capitalize fully on public interest in the topic, but I wonder if we are not risking possible charges of over-commercialisation by adopting your suggestions for the degree ceremony. Clearly gowns are dispensible in these modern times, but it does seem marginally demeaning to ask the chancellor to present degree certificates to a large group of students wearing camouflaged battledress and balaclava helmets. Just a point, you understand."

Scrupulously Costed

Piece rate payment propsed for university teaching. THES, *March 18.*

Ah, Dr Kundel. Do come in. Another term over. eh?

Yes Indeed, Vice-chancellor.

Going anywhere at all for Easter?

Oh, nothing special, sir. Perhaps a couple of days looking at some of the new National Trust places.

Excellent. Now I just wanted to have a word with you about the invoice you've submitted for last term's teaching.

Sir?

No real problems here as far as I can see, although I do notice that you are claiming £9 an hour for the *British Empiricism: Locke, Berkeley, Hume* course.

Ten seminars at £9 per hour.

But surely *British Empiricism* is a grade three course rated at the basic £7.50 an hour. You're not confusing it with *The Vienna Circle and Logical Positivism* are you? I recall that being moved up to grade four last term as a result of national arbitration procedures.

No sir. The extra £1.50 an hour is a special allowance.

31

Special allowance for *British Empiricism?* I think not, Kundel.

No sir. Not for the subject. For "antisocial hours". It's timetabled at 10.15 on Friday mornings.

Ah yes. "Antisocial hours". Silly of me. So that's more or less straightforward then. And I see you correctly claimed the £10 "dirty money" allowance for the *Basic Concepts in Heidegger* course.

Yes indeed.

But there does seem to be one little oddity on your Wednesday morning sheet. I refer to the joint seminar course which you run with Professor Grimethorpe on *The Kantian A Priori.* Now, as a joint course, surely this comes out at just the £6 an hour, whereas you appear to have submitted a figure of £10.

Well sir, if you check below you will see that I have invoked the "single manning" clause: the additional shift allowance of £4.

Could you spell that out a little for me, Kundel?

Well sir, the fact is that Professor Grimethorpe has been a virtual passenger on the course. I was repeatedly required to take the seminar all on my own, and had sole responsibility for making routine philosophical pronouncements during its actual progress.

Good. Good. There doesn't seem to be too much of a problem there. Just one last thing then. Kundel.

What's that, sir?

Rather bad news I am afraid.

Sir?

As you know we've been checking through recent examination scripts in order to establish the exact unit cost of each idea as measured by the initial outlay on teaching. And quite frankly I have to tell you that your course on *Contemporary Advances in Existentialist Thought,* has been declared an "unprofitable seam" and will have to close as from next term. I am sure you understand. But at £3.35 an idea the whole enterprise had become unviable.

Yes sir.

Well that's all for now. Enjoy the break. Oh, and Kundel.

Yes sir?

Don't forget to clock off on the way out will you? Old habits die hard.

Thank you, sir.

Teaching Is Rigorously Evaluated

Performance Indicators for Teaching: A Research Breakthrough?

In their recent joint statement on performance indicators, the CVCP and the UGC express concern about the lack of quantifiable performance indicators for university teaching.

The solution may, however, already be at hand.

This week three Barking social psychologists, Stubbins, Balmer and Baron, have published a major research monograph on the subject *(Stubbins, Balmer and Baron, 1987)*.

The authors give details of a battery of tests which, they claim, capture the two critical but orthogonal factors in university teaching: *Lecturer Performance* (LP) and *Lecturer Competence* (LC).

The test below is taken from the LP range of tests and is published by kind permission of Stubbins and Balmer (Baron was rather unhappy about the whole business).

Please answer the following questions by putting a circle around the response which seems to you to best represent your ideas or feelings on the subject.

1. Which of the following remarks is most likely to be addressed to you at the end of your lecture?

a) I was wondering if you could give me some extra reading on today's topic.

b) I was wondering if I could come to see you to talk further about today's topic.

c) I was wondering if you could tell me how to go about changing courses.

2. It is the third week of your lecture course. When you arrive to give your lecture do you typically think?

a) Gosh, there are more students here than last week.

b) My word, it's nice to see that the numbers are holding up.

c) Perhaps I'd better wait a moment for any latecomers.

3. How long on average are you able to talk in a lecture situation without referring to your detailed lecture notes?

a) Up to 30 seconds.

b) Up to 5 minutes.

c) *What* detailed notes?

4. Halfway through your lecture you realize with a shock that you can't remember what you're talking about.

Do you:

a) Apologize and consult your notes?

b) Ask the nearest student to remind you?

c) Say 'Well, that seems a natural place to stop for this week'?

5. When you glance up from your notes during a lecture are you ever struck by the uneasy thought that.

a) Not a single person is listening to you.

b) You have wandered into the wrong lecture room.

c) You are repeating last week's lecture.

d) The entire audience is about to rush forward and impale you on your epidiascope.

How Well Did You Do?

1986).
Above 65: Senior lecturer material.
Well done.
35 to 65: Proceed beyond the bar.
Below 35: Frankly, you need to pay rather more attention to your lecturing skills. This score means that your present communicative ability is slightly lower than that which was achieved in earlier tests by a lump of wood *(Balmer, Stubbins and Spruce, 1986).*

Next week: Fear and Loathing in the Seminar Situation — the FL Scale.

Research Is Modernized

The Old Department, July 25th

Dear Professor Lapping,
   I'm sorry to bother you again about your research activities, particularly now the weather's taken a turn for the better, but as I explained when I last wrote it is obviously important that this department is properly represented on the university's Three Sides of A4. It is with this in mind that our newly formed Committee for Putting a Good Face on What Looks Like a Very Modest Amount of Departmental Research, has asked me to clarify a few points arising from your recent reply to our Research Activities Questionnaire.

1. Present Publications.
You were good enough to mention two articles which have resulted from your one year's sabbatical leave. These were:
   a) "Reading *Dallas*: the deconstruction of Miz Ellie". *Media, Text and Image.* (Amsterdam) Vol.1. No.1. pp.1-3. b) "The Social Origins of Part-Time Youth Club Leaders". (co-author with Ken Hipstock, Rosemary Wallace and Jose Feliciano) in *The Scottish Journal of Part-Time Youth Club Leaders.* Vol.1. No.1. Page 14.
   Now obviously, we would wish to include these papers in our report to the vice chancellor but unfortunately they appear to be the same articles as were included in last year's report. Would you be so kind as to let us have your comments on this matter. Perhaps they are updated versions of the originals?

2. Favoured Research Techniques.
Under this heading, the Committee decided to make a minor amendment to your own entry, so that it now reads: "Highly detailed and very systematic analysis of an enormously wide variety of written material, including original documentation, specialized archive resources, and relevant data-banks".
   The general opinion in the committee was that this more adequately represented distinctive methodological approach than your own phrase: "Popping in to the library from time to time".

3. Future Research Intentions.

Thank you very much for allowing the Committee to have such a detailed account of your future research intentions. You will recall that you described these in the following manner: *"A Hermeneutic Inquiry into the Theme of 'Nostalgia' in French Culture with Particular Reference to 'Nostalgie de la Boue' in Marcel Pagnol, 'Nostalgie de la Mère' in Marcel Proust, and 'Nostalgie de la Parole' in Marcel Marceau".*

After very careful consideration of this proposal by our newly formed Committee for Making Existing Speculative Research Look Much More Policy Oriented, it was decided by a majority of one that your research might be slightly "refocused" in order to retain your central concern with the past while simultaneously suggesting practical pay-offs. The Committee has accordingly modified the title to: *"The Effectiveness of the Youth Training Scheme in the West Midlands, 1983/5".*

May I take this opportunity of saying how much we all look forward to seeing you next term.

Please pass on my best wishes to Mrs Lapping.

D. QUINTOCK,
Acting Chair.

Meticulously Documented

Dear Vice-Chancellor,

Further to your request of June 22, I am now pleased to enclose a list of the major publications by members of this department in the academic year 1980-81.

Scrunt, Bill (Dr) 'Smash the Bosses Now!' *Big Red Axe,* March 18, 1981.

Clackworthy, Richard (Dr) Contributions to *Penguin Dictionary of Contemporary Political Concepts* 'U-turn'. 'Monetarist', 'Heseltine'. Harmandsworth 1981.

Dreggs, Arthur. Fairly long letter to *The Listener* about lack of buffet service on 7am train from Kings Cross to Doncaster, April 6 1981.

Wincyette, Amanda (Dr) 'Vaginal Cream: Who Cares?'. *Guardian Women.* October 14 1980.

Turncote, Raymond (Prof) 'The Exciting Promise of Monetarism'. *The Economist,* July 3 1980. 'Stop Printing Money'. Aims of Industry Bulletin. September 6 1980. 'Slash Public Spending Now'. *The Daily Telegraph,* November 9 1980. The Attack upon the Universities'. *The Guardian,* January 12 1981. 'Who Killed Robbins', *New Statesman,* March 6 1981. "Not One Job Must Be Lost'. *AUT Bulletin.* May 11 1981.

Prostrate, Jeremy (editor of *Monographs on Sexual Aberrations in Isolated Communities.*) No.1. Mull; 2. Uist; 3. Milton Keynes. *Loughborough Univer-*

sity Press 1981.

Cake, Leonard (Dr) Nothing this year but in fact I've got several things which are likely to come off in the near future. I mean only the other day this chap from Martin Robertson came to see me and said he was "very interested" (not just "interested") in something that I was thinking about in the general area of race relations, you know in cities, and riots and that sort of thing.

Lissom, Fay (Dr) *Ragwort and Daffofils: A Bouquet of Love Poems.* Wilson. Keppel and Betty (Gothenburg) 1980.

Lustgarten, Edwin *Don to a Turn: a Cookery Book for the Discerning Academic.* Olympic Press (Paris) 1981.

Wotan, Thor (Visiting Fellow) 'Ansplogen Krast Diplunskit — Vashacka'. (Thackrick) *Mushmalistaka* Vol.2, No.47 (Draknist).

Weighed

That's two stone, ten pounds and four ounces, Professor Lapping.

Thank you, Maureen. Is that with or without Dr Quintock's thesis?
That's with.

Ah yes. Well, that still means we're only five or six pounds behind Philosophy and quite a few people left to go. Now, what about Mr Odgers?
His pile is just behind you.

Everything here, Maureen? Books, monographs, occasional papers, abstracts of conference papers? It looks a little light.
Nine pounds three ounces, he estimates, but he did send a note as well, saying that on grounds of principle he was refusing to include his doctoral thesis.

Principle?
Yes. He says: "I take the greatest exception to the vice chancellor's idea that the only way for this university to establish UGC research priorities is by resorting to this form of crude quantification."

Have you seen his thesis, Maureen?
I did glimpse it stir, when he took it off the stack.

And what was your honest estimate of it?
I'd say about nine ounces, Professor Lapping. Just one slimmish volume. And no separate boxes of data or addenda or completed questionnaires.

Only a minor setback then. And still no news of Dr Piercemüller's data?
I'm afraid not. It does now look as though most of it was carried out to sea during that freak storm in Deauville.

Pity. But here's all of mine. That's five-and-a-half pounds. And there's this large pile from the research fellows. Another nine-and-a-half-pounds. What sort of a total does that give us?
Altogether. . .it's. . .er. . . four stones, six pounds and seven ounces.

Not bad at all. A whole stone and a half above Philosophy, nearly a stone

clear of Linguistics but still a good half-hundredweight behind Economics. Not bad at all. No grounds for a low research rating there, wouldn't you agree, Maureen?

Yes, sir. One slight problem, though.

What's that?

Well, Professor Lapping. As you know I'm only too happy to take all this over the vice chancellor's office for the final weigh-in. But I do need to make a phone call first.

So, what's the trouble, Maureen?

Well. . . could I put them down for a second?

Costed

A survey on research spending in higher education commissioned by the Department of Education and Science recently produced the following statistics:

1. The *average* cost of producing a research paper in a British university is £12,000.

2. The *average* number of papers produced per member of staff per year in universities is 1.5.

Further quantitative findings from this study are now available:

2. The *average* number of fruitless journeys to the library before the discovery of the exact volume and page numbers of an essential reference in any research paper is 26.2.

4. The *average* number of weeks taken by professional journals to send the author's research article to external referees is 13.6.

5. The *average* number of months taken by external referees to send in their reports to professional journals is 13.6.

6. The *average* number of irrelevant or misleading remarks made by external referees in their eventual reports on research papers is 5.2.

7. The *average* number of suspicions among writers of research papers that at least some of the criticisms advanced by external referees are prompted less by objective scientific criteria than personal maliciousness is 6.2.

8. The *average* number of articles on much the same topic which appea in other journals during the lengthy period in which the author is awaiting publication is 4.3.

9. The *average* number of complimentary remarks made by members of the author's own department upon publication of any research paper is 0.062.

10. The *average* number of requests for copies of any research paper from academics working in related intellectual areas in Britain is *0.1.*

11. The number of requests for copies of any research paper from academics working in related intellectual areas in New Zealand and Holland is *22.6.*

12. The *average* number of occasions upon which those working on any research paper ponder such *averages,* carefully consider the negligible effect that eventual publication will have on their present promotion prospects, and thereupon can be heard to mutter *"Stuff this for a game of tin soldiers"* is *12.8.*

And Backsliders Detected

A Professor Cracknell of Dundee University has proposed a committee to investigate possible "sloth" among staff — THES.

Yes, Dr Piercemüller. Do come in. Welcome to the Lack of Publications Sub-Committee.

Thank you, sir.

Let me first of all introduce the other members. On my right Professor Midlothian — eight books and 47 articles, and on my left Dr Fife — 11 books, two of which are very long, and 53 articles. And then, myself, Professor Stenhousemuir — 19 books and 637 articles. And, of course, our administrative assistant, Mrs Dumbarton, with just the four articles. Is that all clear?

Yes. Thank you very much, sir.

Now as you may know, Piercemüller, this little sub-committee was set up by the General Academic Sloth Committee, and our specific brief is to have a look at all those chaps who haven't published anything whatsoever for the last 20 years. That, I take it, is your present position?

Yes indeed, sir. Nothing at all in the last 20 years.

I wonder then, Piercemüller, if we might ask if you've actually thought of writing anything at all during that time.

Oh yes. I definitely thought of writing a short piece in about 1967.

Good. You'll excuse me pressing the point a little. But I wonder if you could indicate how definite your thought was at the time?

Fairly definite.

Yees. "FAIRLY DEFINITE INTENTION". That's most helpful. And did you by any chance have a clear idea of the possible content of this possible article?

Not the exact content. But a sort of rough idea.

"ROUGH IDEA." That's fine. Now how about a title. Did you make any progress in that area?

Not really, no. But, as I remember, I was quite clear on one aspect.

Yes, do go on, Dr Piercemüller.

I rather thought I'd send the completed piece to *The Proceedings of the Aristotelian Society.*

That's fine. So, "A VERY CLEAR PUBLICATION IN MIND". Anything else at all: perhaps coming up to date a little. Say in the last decade?

Yes, I had another fairly definite idea in about 1976.

Oh good. Could you tell us a little more about that one. What form did it take?

It was critical.

Yees. Good. Critical of what exactly?

My earlier idea.

Excellent. So let's pull that together so that Mrs Dumbarton can put it into a coherent form for the General Sloth Committee. "Two fairly definite but contradictory ideas and one very clear intended journal". Finally, Dr Piercemüller is there anything else you feel we should take into account?

Well, I think that I may be getting round to having another fairly definite idea for an article at the moment.

Oh fine. We can cover that in the usual way I think. Just make an additional note will you, Mrs Dumbarton. "ONE FAIRLY DEFINITE IDEA (in preparation)". Next please.

Bright New Staff Recruited

UGC decision to apply upper age limit of 35 to new blood appointments could be unlawful — THES.

Well, gentlemen, that seems to be the last of our new blood interviews for this morning. Shall we proceed in the usual manner? Jolly good.

Just to start things off, I'd like to come out pretty strongly against Swindon. That was the physics chappie with the red hair and the houndstooth jacket — the UMIST man who seemed a bit confused by my question about the value of moral education. Quite honestly, he didn't strike me as the sort of chap one would want to see in a university, new blood or no new blood.

(Murmurs of "Hear, hear.")

Possibly it was those heavy Alpine boots he favoured, but I did feel that there was a certain loucheness, which didn't quite gel with me. I mean we have to face the fact that this new blood chappie is going to be a bit of a novelty for a few months: he'll have to be wheeled out to make polite conversation at British Council receptions. That sort of thing. And it does seem to me that in those circumstances — where we're all talking about the new information technology and the way ahead — that we could do with someone who looks, how could one put it, well a little less rural.

(Murmurs of "Hear, hear.")

Neither was I greatly impressed by Turnpike. D'you remember him? Physics again — Imperial — nervous — stutter — didn't seem to have heard of Matthew Arnold. Nothing much there I thought.

(Murmurs of "Hear, hear.")

And then that chappie Devizes — Fair Isle sweater under his suit — first class degree - doctorate — sixteen articles already published — very involved in microwave, or at least that general area. Seemed to know his stuff. And just coming up to 22. Although of course, we mustn't be seen to be using age as the key factor. What we've really got to concentrate on is the actual value of the chap as an individual — and there, quite frankly, I have to say that he seemed a shade too pleased with himself. So overall, I'd be inclined to make him a good second.

(Murmurs of "Hear, hear.")

That leaves us with Douthwaite. *Very* impressive, I thought. Mature. Well spoken. Long list of publications. Good administrative record. And just the sort of chappie one wants to find in a university like this.

(Murmurs of "Hear, hear.")

May I then invite him in and let him know of our unanimous decision?

(Murmurs of "Hear, hear.")

Ah, there you are, Douthwaite. Yes, do sit down. Well, I'm very pleased to tell you that after a great deal of careful thought about the matter, my colleagues and I are delighted to be able to offer you the new blood appointment. WELCOME BACK FROM EARLY RETIREMENT.

New Staff Flexibility Encouraged

"Librarians must demand an active role in planning academic courses" — THES.

"May I, on behalf of the Department, formally welcome Mr Buckle, the university's Senior Librarian (Cataloguing), who is here to offer us his invaluable advice on our proposed new second-year course. Mr Buckle."

"Thank you, Professor Eglington. Let me say right away that all of us in Cataloguing, and I'm sure I also speak here for the Bindery, are only too pleased to see a new course in Poetry. For a start, it's an academic subject in which the average book size is commendably smaller than most and therefore such as to make only modest demands upon our precious storage space. But in addition, there is also the gratifying brevity of the actual texts. A great deal of Poetry is quite short enough to allow students to make effective use of our new 30-minute Green Star Loan System. So, all in all, that's a general thumbs up for poetry from the Issue Desk point of view.

"I have to say, however, that a few Reader Service problems do surface when one gets down to the actual poets you intend to cover. While I fully recognize that your new course is entitled *The Pessimistic Tradition in Twentieth Century Anglo-American Poetry,* would it be at all feasible to make do without T.S. Eliot? Quite honestly there's always a heavy demand for Eliot in the spring term, and the situation has only been aggravated in the last academic year by the decision of the Ecology Subsidiary to make *The Waste Land* a set book.

"And if, as I hope, we are in the business of looking for an alternative, then how about good old Pound. Particularly those Cantos. We have multiple copies of each set, but not I'm afraid, a single borrowing since 1965. Just a thought.

"No real problems with the journals you mention. We're still taking *Odin* and *Thetis,* but I have to remind you that *Amphitrite* was cancelled in the last round of cuts and replaced with *The Newfoundland Journal of Occupational Dermatology.* As I recall there was a *quid pro quo* which allowed you to hang on to *Thrust*".

"One other point you might like to bear in mind in designing future poetry courses. Now that we have the University of Alberta's *Poetica Abstracta* in stock, it has become possible to look up substantive poetic topics, say. *Sea Journeys: Accidents,* and then read off the key poems in that area: *The Ancient Mariner, Lycidas, Wreck of the Hesperus/Deutschland.* Once one has this information, then it obviously becomes possible to plan courses around topics rather than individual poets or types of poetry. At the moment, the top poetic subjects in our library as measured by the overall number of lines available are:

a) Well-known birds and their habitats
b) Flowers of the Lake District
c) Reactions to explusion from Paradise

"So something else there to think about."

"Yes indeed. Thank you. Mr Buckle. Most stimulating. Now, you have kindly indicated our readiness to accept questions, with, I understand, one provision?"

"That's right, Professor Eglington. Rather a parochial library tradition. I'm afraid, but I wonder if it would be possible for them to be asked in strict alphabetical order?"

Intellectual Overlaps Detected

Ah Professor Morris. Good to see you. Do come in.

Thank you, Professor Lapping. Actually, it's Morrison.

Really? I do apologize. Well now, may I start by thanking you for coming over to see me.

I though it probably easiest in view of your back trouble.

Ah yes. A long walk. You're more or less on the other side of the campus, aren't you?

True.

Professor Morris, as you will know, there are discrepancies at the moment in the staff-student ratios enjoyed by different departments.

Ours is three times less favourable than yours, I believe.

Whatever the exact figures may be. So we therefore accept that some transfer of resources between departments is only a matter of natural justice. But not, of course, anything which might arouse the slightest suspicion of a — and I think the word has to be used — *a merger.*

It couldn't be further from our minds.

Excellent. So I'm delighted to be able to tell you that after a careful consideration of the intellectual overlaps between your discipline and our own, it was decided at yesterday's departmental meeting that we would from next autumn be prepared to open the doors of our first year lecture series — which we like to call *Introduction 1* — to all your students.

That's very generous, Professor Lapping.

And in addition, we would be prepared to consider the permanent secondment of Mr Ted Odgers to your department, Mr Odgers as you may know, does not agree with carrying out academic research on ideological grounds, so I cannot direct you towards any of his books of articles. But he has an excellent reputation as someone who is able to put across narrow and sectarian ideas in a stimulating fashion.

That's most kind.

And finally, although I'm afraid it has so far proved impossible to obtain the views of the person concerned, we would also be prepared to allow one of our most senior colleagues, Doctor Piercemüller, to move across on a temporary basis for one year. This would however, only be effective from January 1 in view of Doctor Piercemüller's forthcoming sabbatical.

Of course.

Well, this is certainly a most generous and thoughtful offer, Professor Lapping, one which I must say was at least partly envisaged by our own departmental meeting yesterday. In fact, on that occasion we did feel, by a fairly substantial majority, that the present imbalances in resources between our respective departments might best be remedied by a rather more straightforward solution.

Fire away Professor Morris. That's the point of colleagues getting together like this.

Well, we'd rather like to have your photo-copier.

And Praise Given Where It's Due

Academics need to be reassured that their work is appreciated.

Julia Cleverdon, THES.

Doctor Quintock — Derek, my dear Derek — do come in. Yes, come right in. Take the weight off your feet.

Thank you, Professor Lapping.

No, don't sit *there,* Derek. No, take my seat. Good heavens, you deserve a little comfort. It's not every day of the week that one has a review article published in the *British Journal of Media Studies.*

Thank you.

That's it. Lean right back. And do swivel around a bit if you feel like it.

Thank you.

Well now, I expect you've already had quite a day. I understand that your colleagues have been showing their respect for your achievement in the usual way?

Yes indeed. Several of them were kind enough to ask me to autograph their copies of the journal, and there was of course the usual gratifying round of applause when I went down to the SCR for morning coffee.

Good. That's what I like to hear. And outside the department?

Also very kind. The library staff generously invited me over this afternoon to run a short lap of honour round the periodicals section.

Excellent. And some acknowledgement from the vice-chancellor?

Yes indeed. I missed it myself, but I understand there was a three-gun salute from the administrative block at about midday.

Only fitting. And the usual external recognition?

A telegram from Sir Keith.

Predictable, but still a pleasant touch.

That was my feeling.

Well, Doctor Quintock — Derek, my dear Derek — as your head of department, you'll realize that I myself have to rely on more formal, not to say, traditional ways of recognizing your achievement.

Quite so.

So may I first of all shake your hand. Congratulations, Quintock.

Thank you, sir.

And now, if you'll be so good as to pop into the secretary's office you should find something a little special by the filing cabinet.

You mean. . .?

Quite so. Your very own, brand new, bicycle.

CHAPTER THREE

Student Matters

Now that departments and staff are geared to a new era of higher education it is even more important that the students are good enough to play their role.

Grades must be maintained

HELLO.

Oh hello. Is that Professor Lapping?

Yes. Lapping speaking. Who is that?

Crayke, Professor Lapping.

Crayke?

Yes, we met earlier this year. In February.

February. Did we?

Yes, Professor Lapping. At the interview. The open day for sixth formers. You were very impressed with the essay I'd written on language and thought.

Ah yes. Crayke. A fine piece of work I thought. Very impressive. Interesting ideas on metaphor and metonymy.

That's right. And at the end of the interview you were kind enough to offer me 2 Bs and a C.

Yes indeed. Well, Crayke. What can I do for you today?

Well you see, Professor Lapping, I had a bit of bad luck during the actual examination period.

I'm sorry to hear that Crayke. Nothing serious, I hope.

Well not too bad, sir. But my mother passed away on the eve of the first examination. And then my father unfortunately decided to commit suicide just two days later. All of which meant that I was left more or less single-handedly to cope with the seven younger children.

Do go on, Crayke. What are you trying to tell me?

Well, sir. Let me come straight to the point. What with one thing and another I'm afraid that I was only able to obtain one B and two Cs.

Yees.

And. . .well. . . I was wondering, Professor Lapping, if there was any way

you might still consider me for an undergraduate place in your department.

I'm sorry, Crayke, but it does look as though you seriously misunderstand the situation here at the moment.

Sir?

Don't you realise, Crayke, that this is now a straight two Bs and one C department.

Well I thought that what with. . .

And what's more there are four students this year with straight A's. *Four with straight A's.* That's four with 15 points each. Four with fifteen each.

It's just that. . .

And there's only one D in the place and that's a severely handicapped mature student with two A's to go with it. So even there we've got a solid 12 points.

I do quite appreciate all that but I was wondering. . .

All of which means that we've an average A level score for this department of 11.74. *11.74!* That's .63 up on last year.

I just thought that what with the satisfactory interview and the special home circumstances. . .

I'm very sorry indeed to hear your news. Crayke. Very sorry indeed. But we're not talking about individuals here. Oh no. We're talking about something much more important. Do you realize that?

Sir?

We're talking about educational standards.

Interview Techniques Refined

Computer Discriminated Against University Applicants (THES).

So exactly did you make of her?

Well, d'you know, I think I'd be prepared to go as far as B-plus-ish. A most interesting answer on *Silas Marner*. Most interesting.

Yes, very telling. Particularly. I thought, as it seemed to come entirely from her own reading.

That's it. Most refreshing. None of that rote reproduction of A level notes.

Yes, absolutely. A very pleasant change.

But d'you know, what worried me ever so slightly — and I have to be quite frank about this — was that she was going to have her work rather cut out at university looking after that nipper of hers. I mean there's no — well, you know — no father in evidence.

Yeeees.

I mean in a way she seemed — how could one put it — a shade too cavalier about the whole business.

Yeeees.

I actually jotted down "Maternal Feelings" with a question mark at one

stage.

Now one thinks about it there was perhaps the slightest hint of a chip on the old shoulder.

Yeeees.

I mean she did rather snap at you when you asked if she had read any black authors.

That was a trifle disturbing, wasn't it? Particularly as I was trying to gear the question to her, well, you know. . .

Of course you were. Of course you were.

And then there's the old old problem of grades. She may know a great deal about George Eliot and Dickens and Mrs Gaskell and the Brontës, but quite honestly it doesn't look as though she can get it down on paper. Only a very modest C grade.

Yeees. And one does rather wonder if at 26 she's going to be able to settle in with our usual bunch of 18-year-olds.

Someone as articulate as that is going to stick out like a sore thumb.

So what d'you think? Top half of the Waiting List?

I think quite honestly, we've got to go straight for the Reject. Don't want to raise any false hopes.

True. So that's an agreed 'R'. My initial. *There.* And now yours. *Good.*

You know it's funny to think that next year this will be over — that we'll be handing over the entire selection business to a mere computer.

Yeeees. When you think about it, it's difficult to imagine how they're going to build in all the little subtleties of judgement which are so crucial to the whole exercise.

Oh. I expect they'll manage somehow.

New Students Welcomed By Letters

Ah, Professor Lapping.

What is it, Maureen?

You don't seem to have done your usual letter to the new first-years, sir. The one in which you congratulate them on their A level results.

Haven't I?

No, sir.

There's always something isn't there, Maureen? I was hoping to make a start on cleaning my desk this morning.

I'm sorry, sir.

Nor your fault. Not your fault. Well, let's see. How do we start these damn things?

Something like: "Dear First Year", or "Dear New First Year".

Mmmm. I think "First Year" is enough.

Then something like: "We very much look forward to seeing you in the department at two o'clock on October 6."

As soon as that? October 6?

I'm afraid so, sir.

And I've hardly made a start on the backlog. Come on, Maureen. Let's get this out of the way. What next?

We usually say something about it all being a little strange and anonymous and even alienating at first.

Do we?

Yes, sir. And then go on to say that this is inevitable in a large department but that they will find friendly informal contacts quickly develop with tutors.

Yes. Go on.

And that they will soon come to realize that they are not just students but fully participating members of a vital academic community.

Yes.

And that you — that's *you* sir — and your colleagues try to think of students as intellectual partners rather than as passive recipients of knowledge.

Maureen?

Yes, Professor Lapping.

Did we fill our quota this year?

Oh yes, sir. Easily.

A level average?

Right up, sir.

More applications than we can handle?

People begging to get in.

Good God. A seller's market at last! Maureen.

Sir?

Forget the letter.

Sir?

Just dash off a quick postcard threatening to expel anyone who turns up late.

And Speeches

. . .and in conclusion, let me say just this. You have all earned an undergraduate place in one of this country's finest universities, in one of its most broad-ranging, prestigious, and forward-looking departments of Culture and Media Studies. IT IS UP TO YOU HOW YOU USE IT. Thank you. Now, are there any questions before I ask our first year "supremo", Doctor Quintock, to run over the alterations to the timetable? Yes, the woman in the second row with the turquoise hair.

Professor Lapping, if this is such a "broad-ranging" department, then why does it have so few members of staff? My father says that the Government regards departments with less than 12 tutors as non-viable, and that they'll either have to merge or close down completely.

That's a very good point. Yes, it *is* true that we are only a small*ish* department. But we're now in an excellent position to expand. Oh, yes. Once our staff-student ratio moves up from the present 1:18 to 1:23 then according to the vice chancellor's new rules we will automatically qualify for some part-time help which would bring our staff numbers straight up to 5½. So there's no need for any despondency on that front.

Professor Lapping, if this is "one of the finest" universities in the country, then why did my mother see it in a list of third-tier universities which will end up with no research and only low-level teaching?

Another very interesting question. But again no need for anxiety. All this business about universities being graded into three levels is still pure speculation. *Pure* speculation. When did your mother see this list?

Last Thursday.

As recently as that? *Really*. Well, as I say, pure speculation. Right. Next question, please? Yes, the young woman in the Beastie Boys T-shirt.

Professor Lapping, if this department is so "prestigious" then why does my roommate keep telling me that it was graded 'below average" in the UGC ratings?

Ah yes. I'm glad you've brought that one up. *Very* glad. "Below average" — now, how can I put this — "below average" means "below average" on research. And the reason we're "below average" on research is paradoxically because we're "above average" on teaching. All right? Not that we are in any case "below average" on research. *Oh no*. Several of our publications were missed out by the UGC and what's more at least two members of the committee which made the decision were known to have it in for this department. So no cause for concern there, either. Now, could we have a final question?

Professor Lapping, this is only a small technical point, but I was wondering why, if this department is so "forward looking", all your colleagues now had their faces buried in their hands?

Contact Hours Increased

Doctor Piercemüller! Doctor Piercemüller!

What's that?

It's Maureen, Doctor Piercemuller!

Maureen? Where?

Here. Doctor Piercemüller. Behind you. Running down the stairs behind you.

Ah, there you are. My word. couldn't make you out behind all those files.

Oh, Doctor Piercemüller! I'm so pleased to see you.

And you, Maureen. Nice to see you too. You're looking jolly well, you know. Been away?

No, Doctor Piercemüller. I've been here all the time.

Funny. Haven't seen you around at all.

That's because *you've* been away. Doctor Piercemüller.

Possibly. Possibly. Now look, Maureen. I really must dash. Already 10 minutes behind schedule. Blasted woman at Safeways express checkout said I had more than nine items in the basket, and then when I finally get here had to stick the damned car in the Disabled spot and then limp all the way from the car park to fool that new porter.

It's just that some students were looking for you.

Students **you say?** *Students?*

Yes, Doctor Piercemüller. They came into my office while I was tidying up Professor Lapping's first year lectures.

How many, Maureen?

Seven or eight, sir.

You mean — a mob?

No, no, Doctor Piercemüller. Just Seminar Group 2B on the Introductory Saussure course.

And?

Well, they were wondering. . . they were wondering. . .

Out with it, Maureen. It's not like you to stand on ceremony.

Well, they were wondering where you were this morning, Doctor Piercemüller.

Wondering where I was? **What on earth has it got to do with them? My word, what** *is* **happening in this university? First we have that infernal busybody Jarratt scuttling around trying to make the place run like a biscuit factory, clocking on machines in the SCR, time-and-motion men on top of your bookcase, bleepers in everyone's pocket in case the registrar wants a sudden word. And now the** *students* **are demanding details of one's whereabouts. "Wondering where I was" — indeed.**

It's just you were supposed to be taking them this morning.

Taking them, Maureen? Have you gone mad? *Eight students!* **Where would I possibly want to take them?**

You were supposed. . .

Look, Maureen, it really is terribly pleasant to see you around again but I simply must dash now or Mrs Piercemüller will miss her Stretch and Shape class and I'll have to cancel the hygienist for the second time. Let's have a long chat about all this at the beginning of term.

But term. . .

And Maureen. . .

Yes sir?

Take it easy, won't you? **Don't want you losing all the benefit of that long holiday.**

No, of course not.

Ciao, Maureen.

Ciao, Doctor Piercmüller.

Seminar Techniques Modernized

A DES check-list of teaching skills to be tested may include "ability to avoid sarcasm" — *The Independent,* May 1, 1987.

Ah, Mr Balmer. How very nice of you to join us.

I'm sorry I'm late, Doctor Quintock.

No problem at all, Mr Balmer. I mean, for goodness sake, what's 25 minutes between friends. And now you're here we can make a proper start because as I'm sure you remember this is the very week in which you are due to honour us with your thoughts on the relationship between language and cognition.

That's the other thing. Doctor Quintock. I haven't actually written a paper. Only a few notes: I didn't have time to do all the reading.

Perfectly understandable. Why, you can't have had any more than two term's notice of this assignment — barely enough to find the right shelf in the library let alone read one text book.

Shall I start then, sir?

Quite frankly, Balmer, I can't wait. And I'm sure that goes for the whole group. I sense a great deal of bated breath around the room.

Well, I begin by saying that the relationship between language and thought is complex: And then I go on to use the Eskimos as an example.

As an example of what, Mr Balmer? Of frigidity perhaps.

No. Of the relationship between words and thoughts. You know, about them having different words for snow.

Ah yes. Admirably clear.

Shall I go on, sir?

Yes, Balmer, but not too fast. Do take account of your fellow students who are doing such a splendid job containing their enthusiasm for this topic. People like Mr Harley, for example, who is no doubt itching to tell us his views on the Eskimo language. Yes Mr Harley?

I'm afraid I was away last week, Doctor Quintock.

So you were. Harley. So you were. Why, for all you knew we might have been discussing the second law of thermo-dynamics or the arguments for the retention of the Elgin Marbles. So perhaps someone else. Yes, Mizz Turnbull, I see you glancing at your watch. Are we holding you up at all?

No, Doctor Quintock. But it is 12.15.

Quite right. How time flies when one is caught up in the cut and thrust of debate.

Can we all go then, Doctor Quintock?

Yes indeed, Balmer. Although it does mean that we will have to return to your fascinating paper next week when we will, by the way, be joined by an inspector from the DES. Nothing to worry about. It merely means I will conduct this seminar in a slightly different manner.

How do you mean, sir?

51

I may be just a little less courteous and understanding than usual. Is that perfectly clear? Or would it help if I wrote it out in large capital letters?

Attendance Carefully Checked

A Report on Portsmouth Polytechnic by Her Majesty's Inspectorate expresses concern about student attendance levels at seminars — THES.

So, is everybody here?

I think so.

Nobody hanging around outside in the corridor?

No.

Good. Well, let me kick off this week by calling the register. A trifle bureaucratic perhaps, but we don't want to run into any trouble with the old inspectorate, do we? So here goes. *Karen Armstrong?*

Present, Professor Lapping.

Ah yes. Thank you, Karen. *Peter Evanston?* Do we know where he is?

He was here this morning.

Where exactly?

Talking in the coffee bar. Over by the milk machine.

Talking?

Well, you know, Professor Lapping. Laughing and joking. Perhaps he's forgotten the time.

All right. On we go. *Jacqui Leonard?* Any news on her? Yes, Karen?

Still away with 'flu. Can't shake it off.

But isn't this her third successive week?

She's got a different sort now. Different from the one she had originally.

Most distressing. So much work to make up. *Michael Oliphant?*

His chain keeps coming off.

Pardon?

Trouble with his bicycle. Can't get it properly fixed. And he lives miles out.

Another very irregular attender. *Alison Tomkins?*

She's changed course, Professor Lapping.

Changed course?

Gone to psychology. She wants to be a vet and she heard they had some animals.

I don't seem to have any note of the transfer.

She said she'd put it in your pigeon-hole.

I see. *Luke Wainwright?*

He's gone home early for Christmas. He had an identity crisis last Thursday.

Really? Well, that completes the register. Now, Karen, are there any questions you'd like to ask me?

Regular Feedback Provided

The Committee of Vice Chancellors and Principals is lobbying MPs to gain exemption from the Data Protection Act.

Now then, Flintoff. What seems to be the trouble?

It's my assessment mark. On the *Principles of Linguistics* course. It doesn't seem to reflect my work during the last three years.

Let's not get over-excited. What was your exact grade?

Lower second, sir. I was expecting an upper.

Well, that's not the end of the world, Flintoff. Good heavens, no. You could have got a third. Just think about that.

Yes, but you see I haven't been getting on very well recently with Dr Wernitz and I wondered. . .

Oh what nonsense, Flintoff. My word, it really is funny how you students get such silly ideas. No, the truth is we're above such matters as personal likes and dislikes when it comes to assessment. Well above them.

D'you think, sir, just to set my mind at rest, I might hear the actual report from Dr Wernitz?

Well, I don't think it will really help matters. You'd need to have an appreciation of the complicated way in which such remarks are brought to bear upon the grades themselves. The whole system is highly complex.

I'd appreciate it, sir.

If you insist, Flintoff. I'm happy to go through the report with you. There's no secrecy here. Oh no. Mmm. . . As far as I can see it's all quite standard stuff. Dr Wernitz in line with departmental practice first provides a brief psychological assessment.

What sort of thing does he say?

He — erm — mentions that you — let me see — how does he put it? — yes — he mentions that you are — erm — *"A thoroughly nasty piece of work."*

Yes?

Erm — then he goes on, again as is quite customary, to a couple of minor remarks about your general level of academic confidence — which, incidentally, he finds quite high.

How does he put that, sir?

He comments that, *"It's about time someone wiped that stupid know-all look off his face."*

Anything else?

Not really, no. Apart from a short comment based on your first-year work. What's it say? — ah yes — *"Objected to my pipe."*

Thank you, sir.

Of course all this must be kept in context. Remember your final degree grade as determined at the examiners' board is based on a whole range of other matters.

Would it possible to hear about those matters?
Out of the question.
Why's that?
Quite simply, Flintoff, they're of such indescribable complexity that you'd be much better off knowing nothing at all about any of them. And, Flintoff. . .
Sir?
Do wipe that stupid know-all grin off your face.

Student Anxieties Reduced

Look, Alison, I can't really help you unless you're completely frank with me. Now, can I?
No Professor Lapping. I suppose not.
Well then, let me ask you once again. What seems to be the trouble?
It's just that. . . it's just that. . . I don't like the subject any more and I want to transfer to another department.
But surely you knew what to expect when you came to the Department of Culture and Media Studies. You read your prospectus, didn't you?
I thought I'd like it then.
Alison. I want you to listen to me very carefully. Very carefully indeed. Everything seems a teeny-weeny bit frightening to you at the moment, doesn't it?
Well, I. . .
The lectures seem rather disjointed and a little off the subject?
Yes.
And you find that seminars are a trifle dull and the tutor does most of the talking?
Yes.
And the subject itself isn't as exciting or stimulating as you expected?
Yes.
Just as I thought. Alison, I'm going to tell you something. Those feelings of yours are not unique. Oh no. In fact I wouldn't be surprised if most of your fellow first-years felt exactly the same.
Oh.
What you're experiencing, Alison, is a perfectly normal reaction to university education. You see, our teaching isn't designed to spoonfeed you knowledge in the way you were at A Level. What we're introducing you to are not simple truths but ambiguity and uncertainty, irony and paradox. So, of course you feel dissatisfied and disturbed. We wouldn't be doing our job if you felt anything else.
I see.
And what you'll find is that gradually you'll become less rigid and a little

more ready to appreciate — how shall I put it — yes, — the creative mess which is so much part and parcel of education at this level. So, why not go away and think very carefully indeed for a couple of weeks and then come back and tell me your decision.

Thank you, Professor Lapping.

Good. And have you told anyone else about your wish to leave this department?

Only my academic supervisor, Doctor Piercemüller.

And he spoke along similar lines to myself?

He said he was sorry he couldn't do anything to help me at the moment.

Yes?

But if I was forming an escape committee he'd rather like to be chairman.

Students Needs Attended To Even During Staff Vacations

Ello

Ello, Êtes-vous Nice Un-Zero-Six-Sept-Deux-Cinq?

Ah oui.

Vous parlez Anglais?

Non, je regrette.

Eh bien. Pardonnez-moi de vous troubler a cette time de jour, mais est-il possible de parler avec le Docteur Piercemüller?

Comment?

Docteur Pee-airce-mull-aire.

Piercemüller, vous dites?

Oui. Il m'a donné cette nombre de telephone en case d'emergencié.

Et votre nom?

Je suis Maureen, la secretaire du départment où le Docteur Piercemüller est supposé de travailler.

Ah, quel shâme.

Pourquoi vous dites "Quel shame"?

Parce que, Docteur Piercemüller est tres occupé avec ses recherches a ce-moment-le. Il me demande que ne personne le disturber. Quoi exactement est le probleme?

Très serieuse, je suis effrayé. J'avais ici dans mon office un de ces etudiants qui m'a demandé qu'il est remotement possible pour Docteur Piercemüller de marquer et retourner son essai.

Je ne suis pas un grand expert sur les affaires academiques, mais il me parait un peu dehors de ordre de contacter son professeur pendant les vacances longues.

Oui. Peut être. Mais cet étudiant veut utiliser cet essai comme le basis pour

son dissertation de la troisieme année.

Ah, un moment. Je crois que je comprends la raison pour cette state des affaires. Sans doute, Docteur Piercemüller a marqué déjà cet essai mais le retour est delayé par la gréve de la poste en Angleterre.

Je ne pense pas.

Vous sonnez très sure de votre-meme.

Oui, je suis très très sure — parce que l'essai en question est encore dans le trou de pigeon de Docteur Piercemüller dans cet office, ou il a resté dupuis le commencement de la dernière terms. So voilà.

Assurement, vous ne parlez pas le verité. Docteur Piercemüller m'a dit plusieurs temps qu'il est fed aux dents revers avec ces constant attaques sur son administration. Il m'a dit qu'il est assez plein de conscience que tous les autres professeurs quand il vient de completer les assignations.

Vralment? Puis peut-être vous voudrez aimer lui demander où sont ses listes de lisante pour le prochaine terme — ou sont les reportes seminaires pour les trois dernières terms — et où sont ses listes des publications recherches pour les cinq dernières annees.

Sacré Moses! Vous allez trop far. Je anticipai que Docteur Piercemüller sera très dehors de sortes quand je lui conveyè cetté message. Je pense que s'il est harassé sur ses vacances any more, puis il acceptera la suggestion par le vice chancellor qu'il move a un autre departement altogether. Puis vous serez sorry.

Oh, je vois. Celà est votre game. Puis vous pouvez lui reconter de moi qu'll y à un departement ou il sera certainement non bienvenue.

Où exactement?

Le departement de Francais. Bonjour, monsieur.

Bonjour, Maureen.

(With acknowledgements to Miles Kington).

Examination Papers Stringently Checked

Dr Shadbolt, I wonder if you'd be good enough to read out the offending question.

Certainly, sir.

Together with the controversial punctuation.

Of course. This is Question 7 on the Nineteenth Century Popular Culture paper. *Inverted Commas.*

Single or double?

Erm. . . double.

Could be critical. On we go.

Yes. *Double Inverted Commas. Initial Capital.* **The typical function of esoteric cultures within Victorian popular theatre was to provide an**

opportunity. . .

Is there much more of this, Dr Shadbolt?

Just a little. . . erm. . . . was to provide an opportunity for the symbolic loosening of moral imperatives which might have been intolerable within more domestic settings.

Mmmm. Well, is that it?

Not quite. The inverted commas close after "domestic settings", and then we have the additional instruction: "Discuss with reference to the courtship of, *capital,* Nanki, *hyphen* Poo, and, *capital,* Yum, *hyphen* Yum".

I take it that "Poo" and "Yum" are also capitalized.

Yes indeed. Both "Poo" and "Yum" — although perhaps for clarity I should say both "Yums".

Quite. Well, there seem to be several points of interpretation which might be raised by this question, but as you all know this Examination Papers Subcommittee may not address itself in any way to content but only to formal grammatical features, and it is on this aspect that I understand Dr Rackstraw wishes to speak.

Thank you. The problem that I wish to bring to the subcommittee's attention is that this quotation on Dr Bunthorne's paper turns out not *to be a quotation, if that is the word, from Dr Bunthorne himself. This does seem to me to raise the important question of whether or not it should be placed within quotation marks.*

Thank you, Dr Rackstraw. Fortunately though, we have a set of procedures which take care of this situation. First, can we establish whether or not Dr Bunthorne simply invented this convoluted sentence for the examination paper — in which case quotation marks are explicitly excluded — or whether it was taken from written material produced for another occasion.

He claims to have written it nearly two years ago.

I see. Then, under Rule 6(2) it is technically a quotation and qualifies for inverted commas.

But he tells me also, that the paper in which the statement was included has not been published.

Will it be published before the date of the actual examination?

It seems unlikely, sir.

Then under 6(2) iii, only *single* quotation marks are in order. Is that perfectly clear to everyone? *Good.* Now we can turn to item eight on the agenda. *Twentieth Century Popular Culture,* and the problem raised by the use of *single* quotation marks in the question: *Critically examine the demystification of gender differentiation implicit in the recent work of 'Boy' George.* Yes. Professor Pewbar.

Even The Questions Questioned

BACHELOR OF ARTS (BA)
THE THEORY AND PRACTICE OF EXAMINATION SETTING
(PART ONE)

Time Allowed: Three Hours.
Answer Three Questions.

1. Critically evaluate the changing role of the "oral" in the British examination system.

2. Recent advances in Examination Setting Theory suggest that we may soon witness the demise of the familiar instruction — **Answer One Question From Each Section.** Do you agree?

3. Write a short essay on any topic which you have not covered at all on the course but which has nevertheless turned up on the examination paper.

4. What, in your view, are the principal characteristics of the multiple choice examination technique as favoured in some North American universities. Is it:
a. A fairer way of testing candidates' knowledge?
b. A guarantee of objectivity in marking?
c. A technique which readily lends itself to computerization?
d. Conclusive evidence of the mindless nature of American undergraduate life?

5. What, if any, are the advantages of writing on one side of the paper only? (Give examples.)

6. "The harder you look at the words in this quotation from someone called Dawkins, the less sense they seem to make" (Dawkins). Discuss.

7. Outline the methods you would employ to establish the presence (or absence) of plagiarism in the following extract from a recent examination answer:
"In my opinion, it seems to me that, the wealth of those societies in which the capitalist mode of production sort of prevails, more or less presents itself as an immense kind of accumulation of what could be called commodities, its basic unit being basically a single commodity."

8. Critically discuss the relative merits of "Critically Discuss" and "Critically Evaluate". (You may use your log tables.)

9. Write brief notes on any *two* of the following terms:
a. Aegrotat
b. Viva
c. Mitigating Circumstances
d. Doctor's Note

External Examining Taken Seriously

Department of Media and Cultural Studies, 21st June 1989

Dear Professor Dowtidge

I'm writing in my capacity of Examinations Officer to provide you with some background information on a few of the disputed finals papers which we are now pleased to enclose for your adjudication.

Candidate 518247 Spooner J. Examination: Linguistic Theory
As you will see the internal markers have a serious disagreement here. Doctor Piercemüller has awarded a mark of '57', whilst Doctor Quintock prefers an '82'. It is perhaps relevant to this case, although I only mention it for guidance, to say that Doctor Piercemüller has this year displayed what might be called a statistically abnormal predilection for the mark of '57' — having awarded it to thirty-nine out the forty-two papers which have fallen under his purview.

Candidate 529186 Dubbins S.K. (Miss). Examination: Dadaism and After
Although this candidate has performed well elsewhere in her finals papers she appears in this instance to have taken advantage of what her internal examiner called 'a tendency within the subject matter' and submitted eight pages of 'automatic writing'. At first the internal examiner was inclined to rate this as an overall Pass (principally on the grounds that it was relatively long *and* laser-printed) but Professor Lapping subsequently undertook the complex task of comparing Miss Dubbins' work with an earlier example of the genre conceived by a Ms Gertrude Stein. His feeling after this exercise was that Miss Dubbins certainly merited a Lower Second and Ms Stein a borderline Third.

Candidate 543172 Bocock N.V. Examination: Base and Superstructure
This particular paper raises a rather serious issue in that it was originally marked by Mr Ted Odgers, who now, on ideological grounds related to the recent pay dispute, refuses to release his mark. (I should say that this is a localized problem in that Mr Odgers has only this one student on his present 'Base and Superstructure' course). It's difficult to know how best to proceed in the circumstances. Doctor Quintock does claim to have seen the phrase "Remember 68' written in large letters in Mr Odgers Desk Diary but given Odgers historical interests, this may well refer not to Bocock's paper but to the 'events' of '68. Professor Lapping has, however, now proposed that we proceed on the assumption that the paper has been marked by another internal examiner — namely, Doctor Piercemüller — and that it therefore be regarded as a '57'. We look forward to your comments on this sensitive matter.

I think all the other twenty-seven problem cases which I'm forwarding to you along with these remarks are more or less self-explanatory, and I very much look forward, as do all my colleagues, to seeing you at our Examiners Meeting the day after tomorrow.

Best Wishes

L. Turpitz (Examinations Officer-*still*)

Plagiarism Rooted Out

"Academics are lazy at detecting cheating". Conference report, THES.

Shall we start at the beginning, Professor Lapping?
What's that, Doctor Wernitz?
At the beginning of Prudom's script.
Prudom?
To check for plagiarism, Professor Lapping. You remember the board's decision?
Oh yes. Quite right. Do excuse me, Doctor Wernitz. My mind is on other things. You know, that damn split vote on the word processor committee, compiling a definition of "financial exigency" for the bursar. That sort of thing.
Quite so, Professor Lapping. It's only that. . .
Yes, yes. Do fire away.
Right you are, sir. Now I've underlined the second sentence of the third answer because it does seem on the face of it a trifle problematic.
Come to the point, Werntiz.
Well, sir, it does read a little strangely. Yes, here we are: "The notion of the subject of the enunciation refers to the existence of exopheric pronouns which founds the nature of discourse as the setting up of specifically located subject positions".
Well, that sounds pretty coherent to me, Doctor Wernitz. After all, we are dealing with a question on the relation between semiology and psychoanalysis. Nothing much wrong with that answer. Very much on the right lines, I would have said.
No, sir. You miss the point. My suspicion is aroused by the contrast between that excellent point and the sentence which precedes it.
Do get a move on, Wernitz.
Well, sir, the preceding sentence reads: "This is a very difficult subject but I think in my opinion anyway that it is very important."
Yes, that is a trifle loosely phrased. But satisfactory, Wernitz. Satisfactory.
And then on the next page, sir, the second paragraph, we have this sentence: "The process of production of representations and subjects for these represen-

tations is clearly reinforced by material apparatuses". Now what d'you think of that?

Sounds fairly straightforward, Wernitz. As these things go.

Ah, but, listen to this from the standard text on Language and materialism: "This PROCESS OF PRODUCTION OF REPRESENTATIONS AND SUBJECTS FOR THESE REPRESENTATIONS IS REINFORCED BY certain MATERIAL APPARATUSES." Absolutely identical except for three words.

Well, Wernitz, I concede there's a similarity, but then one *is* dealing with fairly standard concepts: "processes", "production" "representation", "subjects", and "material apparatuses". You can't suddenly start calling them by other names like "marmalade". No, I think this sounds of original enough to be given the benefit of the doubt.

But, Professor Lapping. What possible grounds can you have for such a view? Are you seriously saying that this is original work?

More or less, Wernitz, more or less.

Good heavens.

You see one musn't drive oneself into a corner over these matters, Wernitz. There are serious implications for academic scholarship in general. Always remember that the original writer is not he who refrains from imitating others, but he who can be imitated by none. Yes indeed.

Are those your own words, Professor Lapping?

More or less, Wernitz. More or less.

External Examiners Fêted

Maureen, whatever else you do today, remind me to have a word with *The Maharaja.*

Who's that, Professor Lapping?

It's not a person, Maureen. It's a restaurant. The venue for our departmental dinner on June 23 with the external examiner. I assume that numbers for the event are satisfactory.

On the satisfactory side of things.

Derek Quintock will be there?

No exactly *there*, Professor Lapping. He sent a note yesterday saying that he was very much looking forward to the event — his exact words were — oh yes — "What could possible be more relaxing at the end of a fortnight of sustained marking then settling back for two and a half hours with one's colleagues and the external examiner in the exotic ambience of a tandoori restaurant?" But he goes on to add that unfortunately his wife appears to be going down with a recurrence of the swamp fever she picked up during last year's sabbatical in Oslo.

Most distressing. I take it that Odgers will be there?

Not an absolute certainty. He also told me of his enthusiasm for the evening but then gave me the unhappy news about his recent allergy test.

Allergy test?

It seems that his chronic listlessness is directly attributable to the inhalation of those small wool particles which feature so prominently in the restaurant's decor. Says he just couldn't risk it. Might keel over.

Pathetic. And Piercemüller? Have you seen him since Easter?

He did phone. But the old back's playing him up a bit. He's apparently never quite got over that nasty fall from a pinoli tree in Tuscany last November. If he sits still for longer than 15 minutes he locks into the seated posture.

Couldn't he take a stroll between courses? A couple of poppadoms, a brisk turn round the block, and he'd be fighting fit for the lamb pasanda.

It seems not.

And you, Maureen. How about you?

Oh gosh, I'd *love* to come. But it is rather — well — the wrong time of the month for me. Much as last year.

Maureen, this is all deeply disturbing. What on earth is going to be the external examiner's view of this department when I ring him tomorrow and tell him that every single member apart from myself is unable to dine with him for medical reasons?

Oh well, Professor Lapping, you never know your luck. He might propose an aegrotat.

Even More Care With Selection At Graduate Level

Adam Smith Institute proposes that 'students should work their way through college' — THES.

Yes, do take a seat, Mr Halliwell. My name is Gothard, Professor Gothard as in the pass, and your other interviewer is my good colleague, Doctor Rhinestone. Perhaps I might start by asking you to outline the general theoretical ideas which lie behind your proposed PhD thesis. I understand that it is basically deconstructionist in tone?

That's right, sir. What I wish to do is explore Derrida's anasemiological deconstruction of semiology with particular reference to the problem of meaning as dealt with by Frege and Quine.

Jolly good. Well, let me now hand over to Doctor Rhinestone for some detailed questions.

Thank you, Bernard. Now, Halliwell, I want to come straight to the point and ask you how you'd tackle the persistent problem in this unversity of removing vomit from student mattresses.

I'd definitely start by removing any surface deposit.
Good. Go on.
Then I'd sponge with a warm washing up liquid solution. Then sponge again with water to which a few drops of ammonia had been added.
One moment, Halliwell. Not so fast. Not so fast. You said 'sponge with water'?
Yes.
Hot or cold water, Halliwell?
Erm. . . cold?
Excellent. Well answered. Now, Professor Gothard, perhaps you'd like to follow up that point.
Indeed. I rather want to move away from the topic raised by Doctor Rhinestone but nevertheless to stay within the same analytical area.
Let me set you the following poser. You are cleaning out the Vice-Chancellor's private toilet and find that you have no access to any proprietary cleaner. Neither, for the sake of argument, is there any vinegar immediately available. How would you cope?
I think. . .
Do take your time.
I think I'd try and borrow a couple of denture tablets.
I'm forced to say that those do sound, conceptually, not unlike a proprietary cleaner.
Then, I'd. . . I'd. . . yes. . . I'd pour a glass of coca-cola down the toilet and leave it overnight.
Splendid. Splendid. Most impressive, Halliwell. Most impressive. I think I can tell you here and now that you'd be most welcome in this department.
Thank you.
And all we need now is confirmation of your upper second degree and the answer to the inevitable question for students wishing to study at this advanced level. You do, I take it, have your own mop and bucket?
(with acknowledgements to 4,000 Things You Really Ought to Know by Ginette Chevallier)

Close Graduate Supervision

PhD supervisors criticized for spoon-feeding students, encouraging conformity and discouraging independence — CIBA foundation Seminar, January 1989.

Ah Flintoff. Do come in. Have a seat.
Thank you, Doctor Quintock.
Well, you'll be pleased to hear that I've had a look through the first draft of Chapter Two of your thesis and I can tell you that on the whole it's more

or less on the right lines.

I wasn't absolutely sure whether it would be Chapter *Two*.

Yes, it *is* Chapter *Two*. Quite definitely.

Really?

Oh yes. Chapter *One* is your Introduction. Right?

I suppose so.

Then Chapter 2, Review of the Literature; Chapter 3., Methodology; Chapter 4, Results; Chapter 5, Treatment of Results; Chapter 6, Summary and Conclusion. Then a 15-page bibliography, two appendices, a sample of your questionnaire, and Bob's Your Uncle!

It's only that as my thesis was partly about deconstructionism, I had the, perhaps slightly naive, idea that it might at least partly make the point by deconstructing the traditional thesis format.

Let's not run before we can walk, eh, Flintoff? Now down to a few specifics. I see you criticize Wasserman rather heavily.

You thought my comments unreasonable?

Not exactly. But, you see, we do have old Lomax down as your external and he's very much a Wasserman person.

I see.

And then you do spend an enormous amount of space — nearly three sides — on Burbidge.

He did strike me as a critical link between the two phases of neo-structuralism which I've tried to identify.

All very fine, Flintoff, if you had five years to play with — but when we're talking about having this little package all bound up and in the library within the three-year time limit then two paragraphs is quite enough for anyone.

I'll change that straightaway.

Excellent. And then a couple of minor stylistic points. At the beginning of the chapter you say: "I will start by looking back at a number of earlier studies". I'm not too keen on that personal "I".

I'll correct that.

And "looking back" sounds — well — a trifle casual for a thesis.

I suppose so.

And I'm not too sure about the phrase, "earlier studies". It's a little slack.

I'd certainly welcome your suggestions.

Excellent. You have a pen?

Indeed.

Right. Off we go. "Pre — vious re-search has shown. . . "I'm not going too quickly for you?

No Just right, Doctor Quintock. Thank you very very much.

Overseas Students Given Special Attention

Professor Lapping! Might I have a word?

Ah, Abdul. Keeping well? Settling in nicely? Jolly good. Must dash.

Abd*ou*, Professor Lapping Abd*ou*.

Ah yes. Well, Abdou, what seems to be the trouble? Good heavens, is that the time?

It's my essay, Professor Lapping. I'm afraid I do not understand all your comments.

Cultural differences, Abdou. A grey old world without them.

I do not understand, for example, the meaning of this 'Sp'.

Spelling, **Abdou.**

Spelling?

That's it. Glance across the line and you'll see I've underlined the misspelt word so you can go and look it up and get it right next time. Simple as that.

I see. And then *here,* and *here.* and *here,* you have written something which looks like "Pu".

Punctuation. **Abdou. Punctuation. Some basic fault or other. Could be almost anything: need for a comma, incorrect use of a colon, faulty apostrophes. Try reading your work out loud to yourself. That often gives a clue. Now, I really must dash.**

I see. And then I do not understand all these other signs — the upside down "v"s.

Quite straightforward. They mean something or other has been missed out — a word, an idea, a reference. Whatever.

Ah. And then there are these question marks. All by themselves.

They mean that I'm not too clear about what you're saying — that it is, *literally*, questionable. Now. . .

And then I do not quite make sense of your other comments. On this page you say "Are you sure?", over here you say "Really?" and "Does this follow?" and here on the last page, "Can this be true?"

Should have thought they spoke for themselves, Abdou. Good heavens, is that the time.

Professor Lapping, perhaps I am taking a little longer to settle down than some other overseas students, but I do wonder if your marking might ever be a little more — well — helpful?

"Helpful", Abdou?

Well, instead of saying over and over again that my things were wrong — could you ever spare a moment to tell me what would be *right?*

Good, God, Abdou! Whatever next? Spoonfeeding?

Doctorates Refined

Dear Professor Suckling (Ted),

Thank you for agreeing last July to act as external examiner for the PhD dissertation by E.R. Langridge: *The Social and Psychological Effects of Long-term Unemployment in Rural and Urban Communities*. I am now very pleased to enclose the completed thesis for your assessment.

Obviously at this delicate stage of the proceedings it would be professionally unethical to comment on the standard of this thesis (although I can tell you in confidence that the internal examiner. Doctor J. Noakes, who should know what he's talking about, thinks that it is an absolutely clearcut pass) but may I offer one or two small points of clarification.

Langridge originally intended to look at the social and psychological effects of unemployment in *both* rural and urban communities, and this interest, as you will see, is splendidly reflected in the first four lengthy chapters in which he incisively reviews the relevant empirical and methodological literature.

It was at this point in time, however, that our newly formed Doctoral Deadline Committee considered Langridge's overall progress and decided with reluctance to recommend a slight modification of his fieldwork in order to ensure that the thesis was successfully completed within the four year period.

In brief, it was suggested to Langridge that he might concentrate solely on urban communities instead of urban and rural, and that this might best be restricted to one urban community rather than the three envisaged, and preferably one to which he enjoyed good access, namely his own locality, or as it was subsequently defined for the sake of methodological precision, the people who lived next door to him.

This narrower but more refined focus of research did necessarily mean that some of the variables which Langridge wished to study comparatively had to be excluded: such matters as class, age, sex and ethnicity. Neither was he fully able to explore the entire range of social and psychological effects — suicide, clinical depression, drug addiction, crime, and alienation — in that not one of these was present in his new sample.

It is largely these revisions which have led Langridge to modify his original thesis title. He felt, and I must say I respect his wishes in this matter, that it would now be misleading for him to use a title which was so explicitly comparative. He has accordingly renamed his thesis: *Two Unemployed Students In My Street Who Don't So Far Show Any Major Effects of Unemployment*.

I look forward to hearing what I am certain can only be good news for Langridge, for social science, and of course, last but by no means least, for this department.

All the very best to you, your charming wife, and your delightful children.

G. LAPPING (PROFESSOR)

Time Left For Relaxation

(An alcove in the Union bar.)

Shall I get a drink, Professor Lapping?

No, no, Martin. The drinks are on me today. Oh yes. Special treat. Christmas comes but once a year and all that. But what you can do is pass around this card so that everyone in the group can write down their favoured beverage. That'll save some time. All right?

Yes. Thank you, Professor Lapping. Thank you very much.

And while you're doing that, let's have a bit of quick feedback on the course so far. Yes, Tracey. How has the course seemed to you — apart from all the anxieties associated with being away from home for the first time. D'you think you've settled in? Started to enjoy your studies? Found the lectures stimulating, Eh?

Well. . .

Now come along. Speak absolutely frankly. Try to pretend that I'm not here. Just be yourself. That's the whole point of these informal gatherings.

Well. . . it's been all right.

No major criticisms?

Not really . . . no.

Excellent. That's what I like to hear. And how about you, David?

Me sir?

Yes, you.

I'm Robert, sir.

Of course. Of course. Well, Robert, how did you find the general content of the lectures?

The general content?

Yes, that's right. The overall subject matter. The range of topics.

Oh, that was okay. . . it was. . . yes. . . okay.

Good, good. And Nicholas — or Nick, isn't it? Did you find that the material in my lectures was well-organized? Tightly structured but still nice and clear? Just say if you didn't. What I'm after is some sense of your real feelings on these matters. A bit of honesty.

Well, Professor Lapping. . .

Yes. Any definite criticisms? Something specific? Something which could be changed next time?

Erm. . . no. . . not really.

Pleased to hear it. Very pleased to hear it. Well, Amanda, how about you? Have you got something out of the seminars? Found that they're given you a better grasp of the issues?

Oh yes I. . . erm. . . think. . . erm. . . that's. . . erm. . . that's right.

That's good news. And you Linda? Found that you've had a chance to participate in a meaningful way?

"Oh. . . erm.. . . yes, sir.

Well, I must say, this looks as though it's been a good term for all of us. I've certainly enjoyed teaching you all and it's nice to hear that you feel much the same about being taught. That's the value of feedback. Well, on to less intellectual matters. Time for drinks. Yes, Caroline, what's the order?

Twelve bags of cashew nuts, eight Castellas, and eleven large brandies, please, Professor Lapping.

New Attention to References

'Too often references for graduates. . . reveal little knowledge of the students', Speaker at CNAA national conference on employment.

Come on, Maureen. Leave the decorations to Doctor Quintick. Let's make a start. Who's first?

Geoff Keating, Professor Lapping.

Right. Dear Sir. Re, colon, Mr G. Keating. Paragraph. I am very pleased to write in support of the above named candidate's application for the post of. . . what job is it this time, Maureen?

Probation officer in Hartlepool.

Ah yes. . . for the post of probation officer in Hartlepool. As you will no doubt have already learnt from his application form, Keating graduated from this university in. . . was it '83?

'79.

Tempus fugit. . . graduated from this university in 1979 with an upper second degree in cultural and media studies. This result was generally thought by his tutors to be an accurate reflection of his overall academic abilities. There can be no doubt. . .

Professor Lapping.

Maureen, not when I'm in midflow.

But it was a third.

Then change it to a third. Now, as I was saying. . . an accurate reflection of his overall academic ability. New paragraph. It is only fair to say that Keating took a little time to settle into this department but by the end of the first year, his tutors were impressed by his increasingly mature attitude.

Is "increasingly mature" quite right?

Please don't quibble, Maureen. It's the standard phrase.

But he was nearly 35 by the end of his first year.

Keating?

Yes.

Well, change that to "first term". New paragraph. Although not exactly what one might call an academic "high-flyer", Keating proved himself to be an extremely conscientious and thoroughly trustworthy individual in all his dealings with staff and fellow students.

Cannabis.

What?

He was done for selling cannabis. In the second year. Three months suspended.

George Keating?

Geoff Keating.

Small dapper chap with short hair and a stutter.

Big strapping fellow with a bright orange Mohican and acne.

Better leave out the "thoroughly". Last paragraph. You will no doubt have many applicants for such an interesting position. But, in my opinion, this relatively young graduate is certainly well worth your serious consideration. I am happy to recommend him to you without reservation. Yours, etc, etc. Maureen what on earth is the matter with you now?

Oh, it's nothing, Professor Lapping. Just a small personal dilemma. I was simply wondering whether after all that you'd prefer "sincerely" or "truly".

Don't try to be facetious. Maureen. It doesn't suit you. Now, who's next?

Contacts Maintained With Ex-Students

(New efforts by universities to establish contact with former graduates).

The Provost's Lodge, April, 1989.

Dear Mike,

Well, my word we've been having some pretty bad weather for this time of year, haven't we? I know that our head gardener, "Old Blossom" Craddock (remember him by the way? What a character!), was only telling me the other day that he's not seen an April like this for "many a long year".

But down to business. The real reason I'm writing, Mike, is to invite you (and of course your lady wife, if there is such a lucky person) to the next meeting of our newly formed Alumni Society.

This year's function will take the form of a Grand Reunion Dinner to be held in the partitioned section of the Bertrand Russell College Dining Hall (if you remember that's the section where the final examinations were held). Inclusive price for the dinner and the rest of the evening's entertainment is a very reasonable £47.50. The college chef (yes, old "Scraps" Wainwright himself. Still going strong) has selected the following menu:

Hot Grapefruit

Haddock Bonne Femme
or
Tandoori Hake
served with

69

Sprouts Nicoise
Sweetcorn Mornay
Game Chips

Fresh Gooseberries with Kirsch

The price also includes two (2) glasses of our specially bottled "Campus Wine". (Many people who've tasted this since it was introduced just two months ago have commented favourably upon its distinctive label.)

I am delighted to tell you that for our after-dinner speaker we have been lucky enough to secure the services of one of our more illustrious old boys — Geoffrey Lackpace, MP — who will give a fairly lengthy but relatively disorganized talk entitled "Nooks and Crannies in the House of Commons Library". After dinner we will adjourn for drinks in the Henry Moore Extension Building.

The entertainment for the evening will conclude with a specially devised Son et Lumiere presentation of "The 1969 Occupation of the Administrative Block" which features the recorded voices of the Deputy Registrar, three former student militants, and Detective Inspector Grantley.

Throughout the evening the Bursar and the Deputy Bursar will move discreetly among the guests selling raffle tickets and photographic views of the Albert Schweitzer Concert Hall in aid of the fund to provide serving academics with additional money for travel to overseas conferences.

All the very best from your old friend.

W.R. LEVINGTON
Provost
(or — to use the nickname which, I understand was much favoured by your year — "OLD GOEBBELS")

Stresses and Strains

In this new thrusting entrepreneurial climate there are inevitably casualties.

Some long for former times

Ah Lytham. There you are. Don't stand on ceremony, lad.
Fleetwood, sir.
What's that?
Fleetwood sir. Not Lytham.
Really. Oh well, never mind. Come on in. Grab a chair. That's the way.
Thank you Professor Lapping
Now, what seems to be the trouble. A nasty touch of mid-winter blues
— personal problems — a backlog of essays? Out with it.
Well, it's a little difficult to put into words, sir.
Come along. Spit it out. And do wipe your eyes. No blubbering here. Eh?
Should be ashamed of yourself. Big boy like you. Nice and grown up. Right?
Yes, thank you sir. I'm. . . I'm sorry.
That's better. Now pull yourself together and tell me what's the matter.
**I'ts just that I seem to be. . . sort of. . . overcome by a terrible feeling
of. . . I don't know how to put it, sir.**
You're putting it splendidly. Cleethorpes. Splendidly. Just relax and let
yourself go. You'll find I've got pretty broad shoulders. Now what sort of
"feeling" exactly?
**It's a sort of feeling, sir, that the university isn't any longer what I ex-
pected it to be.**
Good heavens. What on earth did you expect? Milk and honey? Ivory
towers?
**No sir. . . but I thought. . . well, I thought that being in a university would
put me in touch with ideas. You know, sir. Thoughts.**
So it can. But a lot of it's up to you, you know. Oh yes. There's no spoon-
feeding here. You're not at school now.
**I imagined that I'd somehow get mixed up with teachers who wanted
nothing else but to find things out about the world.**

Pure idealism. Heysham. No wonder you're in the state you are. You must take a more practical perspective.

I wanted a bit of enthusiasm and adventure. I know I may be speaking out of turn, but I wanted something more than a place where the teachers all seem so old and tired.

Yes. Go on.

And where they. . . well. . . where they seem to spend most of their time trying to attract second-rate foreign students.

Yeees.

And counting up A level scores and calculating the relative employability of their undergraduates.

Have you finished?

And issuing notices about recently cancelled periodicals.

Quite finished?

And talking sadly among themselves about the promotion they might have enjoyed had the cuts come just that little earlier.

Quite quite finished?

It's as though the spark had gone out. As though an ideal had slowly died in front of their eyes.

Now look here Morecambe.

Sir?

That's all very fine and rhetorical.

Sir?

But do you think you could do me one small favour? Just one?

Sir?

Could you pop back and see me tomorrow about this matter? It's just that. . .

Sir?

It's just that I find it rather difficult to talk with all these damn tears running into the corners of my mouth.

Others Worry About Ageing

Average age of academics continues to rise. *THES*.

Happy birthday, Doctor Quintock.

Er, thank you, Maureen.

It is today, isn't it?

Oh yes. I'm afraid so. Forty-five very average years.

Hardly average, Doctor Quintock. You're a very distinguished person. I was only reading the other day. . .

No, Maureen. You misunderstand me. Not that kind of average. Average *age*. Forty-five is the average age in this department.

I don't see how that. . .
And in the university, Maureen. Forty-five is the average age in the university.
But that doesn't mean that. . .
And in all the universities in this country put together, Maureen. Forty-five is now the average age for all the university teachers in the country.
It's only a statistical thingy. It doesn't. . .
And listen, Maureen. Listen to this. Ten years ago. Ten whole years ago. In 1976. The year of Entebbe and Callaghan and Fred Mulley. Yes, Fred Mulley. Ten years ago. I was the average age as well.
That was hardly your. . .
And 18 years ago, Maureen. Back in 1968. Well before your time. Danny Cohn-Bendit. The Sorbonne. Ted Short. Yes, Ted Short. The very year I started here. The youngest person in the department. *But still I was the average age.*
You mustn't blame. . .
And what's more, Maureen. What's more. In 2001. *Space Odyssey* year, Maureen. *Also Sprach Zarathustra.* When I'm 60. Will I be merely 60? My own personal 60? No, I will not. I will still be the average age. *An average 60.*
But, Doctor Quintock. There'll still be some consolation.
What? Where?
Well. . . you'll still be the youngest person in the department.

Others About Cultural Change

"I think we've come a long way away from the late 1960s, early 1970s when a young revolutionary said to me: 'This is a fun place, man'." — Keele University administrator quoted in *The THES*.

Scene. Somewhere near the administrative block, Keele University.
Hi, there!
Hi!
Hey man, you look really out of your head.
Oh yeah.
Really spaced out.
Well it's this scene, man. You know what this place is?
Tell me, man.
This is a fun place, man. *This is a fun place.*
Yeah?
I just had this really beautiful trip.
With some chick?
Yeah man. She came back to my pad, you know, and we really, like, you know, we really turned on.
Wow!

Yeah. . .
That sounds really mind blowing, man.
Too much. . .
You two getting it together?
No, man, it could get heavy. Know what I mean? Really heavy.
Yeah. . .
I gotta find myself some space. Do my own thing.
Oh, yeah.
I don't want any hang-ups, man. No hassle. No bad vibes.
Yeah, well, remember, tomorrow's the first day of the rest of your life.
Wow, that's beautiful. Really beautiful. . .
And hey, man.
Yeah?
In case I don't see you around the campus any more.
Yeah?
Best of luck with your early retirement.
Hey, yes. And you with yours.
Let'a make some really good karma with the old lump sum.
Far out.
(Exit left pursued by fully-clothed students.)

And Physical Fitness

"Chinese academics are the target of a new keep-fit campaign" — THES.

THE FIRST NATIONAL UNIVERSITIES GAMES
(Sponsored by United Biscuits)

Event 1.
Grand 3 x 24 hrs Relay Race
In this exciting race against time, the baton — a 47-page UGC questionnaire
on teaching loads and staffing levels — is first passed to a registrar who holds
it at arms' length for 24 hours before handing it over quickly to a vice
chancellor who in turn hands it straight back to the registrar who must then
run round in ever descreasing circles for a further 24 hours before handing
it back to the UGC (n.b. *No members of academic staff are allowed to touch
the baton at any time during this event).*

Event 2.
High Vaulting Competition
(Open to all New Blood lecturers)
In this novel test of athletic prowess, an uninterrupted row of middle-aged
academics is pegged at the top of the scale. The winner of the competition
is the new blood lecturer who can successfully vault over this row while

trampling on the least number of sensibilities.

Event 3.
Tug-of-War
In this event, which is only open to local authority representatives and directors of polytechnics, both sides endeavour to tug a bike shed (or other disputed property) into their own territory to the accompaniment of such shouts as:
'You gave it to us in '56'
'No, we only lent it to you'
'If we can't have the bike shed you can't use our car park'
'Who said it was *your* car park?'

Event 4.
100m each way sprint
(Open to past or present Government Ministers with responsibility for higher education)
Competitors will be required to run very quickly in both directions at precisely the same time while chanting 'Britain Needs Its Universities' and 'Close the Buggers Down' (n.b. *There are no winners in this event*).

Event 5.
3 x 12 month marathon
Teams of already overburdened academics will endeavour to carry an oddly assorted bunch of doctoral candidates over a standard PhD course within the minimum qualifying time of three years. Those supervisors who fail to complete the course in time — irrespective of the weight of their candidate — will be immediately disqualified from all future competitions.

Event 6.
Marksmanship: Clay Pigeon Shooting
(Open to vice chancellors only)
On a given signal a small number of ageing philosophers will be released from their coops. The winner will be the vice chancellor who is the first to 'bag' a philosopher with a fusillade of false syllogisms, chop-logic and *ad hominem* arguments.

There Are Ideological Strains

"Oh, do excuse me, Doctor Quintock. I saw your door was open so. . ."
 No problem at all, Doctor Lesnoff. Do come in. Have a seat. How are you settling down in the department?
 Very well indeed, thank you.
 Managing to ride all those "new blood" jokes.
 Jokes?
 You know — "if you're the new blood lecturer how about a quick transfu-

sion" — that sort of thing.

Ah yes. Very good. No, what I wanted to see you about was rather different: I understand that you're well, the AUT shop steward for this department.

Oh good God no. Not "shop steward". Oh no. I've sort of agreed on a more or less temporary basis to be the sort of departmental chappie for the AUT — you know, the man who circulates the odd handout or two, takes the occasional phone call.

But you do know all about the assessment boycott?

Boycott?

Yes.

Well, you know, I wouldn't exactly call it a "boycott". "Boycott" is such a negative term, isn't it. So definite.

But it is union policy not to take part in any student assessment?

That's certainly the general import of the union's present policy. But I do have to tell you that an awful lot of AUT members up and down the country didn't actually vote at all in the ballot and that quite frankly even among those who did there are quite a few who don't necessarily feel it's the best way of going about things.

I see.

But if you are a member of the AUT. . .

I am.

Well then, if after you've carefully examined your conscience over this matter, and made allowances for the few special cases which crop up — you know, the odd bits of assessment here and there which no one will notice too much — then perhaps you might consider, and I'll put it no more strongly then this, you might consider not undertaking too much assessment work until we get the okay from the union bigwigs.

Thank you, Doctor Quintock.

And Lesnoff.

Sir?

Perhaps you'd be so good as not to mention my off-the-cuff comments about the AUT to any other members of this department.

Of course.

You see, strictly between ourselves, most of them don't quite go along with my militant stance.

Feelings Of Not Being Appreciated

Now look, I'll tell you something you didn't know. I'll tell you something. . .

Darling. . .

No. You listen. I just want to say one thing. Just one thing.

Darling, I'm sure the Vice-Chancellor doesn't want to hear. . .

Because, you see, this year things are going to be different.

Are they, Doctor Wernitz?

Oh yes they are, Vice-Chancellor. You mark my words.

Vice-Chancellor, you must excuse. . .

I'll tell you what. You think — you all think — that I'm just a clapped out old academic, don'tsha?

Really darling, nobody. . .

Shtuck at the top of the lecturers' shkale for six years. And shtuck there for another ten years or until the AUT abolishes shenior lecturers altogether. That's what you think, isn't it, Vice-Chancellor?

Not at all, Doctor Wernitz. Your overall contribution to the university is highly valued.

Old clapped-out Wernitz. That's what you think. Look at the poor old bugger's C.V. One co-written out-of-print text book, two articles in *New Society* and one review-in-brief in *TLS* and that's his lot. If it wasn't for the wonders of tenure you'd have had me down the road with my cards in my hand before the Bursar could say "premature retirement". Right?

Darling, do get your coat. I'm sure the Vice-Chancellor wants to spend some time with his other guests.

But let me tell you this. Old clapped out Wernitz is the only one to see the reality behind this university.

Well, Doctor Wernitz, that's very intriguing, but. . .

I see the irony. And the paradoxes. And the alienation. And the anomie. Oh yes.

You do?

Oh yes. And this year — this very year — 1988. . .

1989, darling. We just sang Auld Lang Syne to 1988.

That's what I said. 1989. This year I can see it all. Nothing escapes me. Cut through to the heart of the whole farce. Expose the raw nerve. Subvert the rituals and convenshions. Hold a mirror up to nature.

Look, Vice-Chancellor, I really must apologize on Doctor Wernitz's behalf. It's just that. . .

And then they'll remember me. Old top-of-the shkale Wernitz.

It's just that every New Year's Eve he goes through this personality change.

They'll say to themselves: "Remember all those departmental meetings when we used to think he was asleep."

You mean a sort of alter ego?

More dramatic than that. He becomes a being, who by the exercise of

special powers, is able to transcend the material conditions of his own existence.
You mean?
Exactly. Every New Year's Eve after a litre of Hirondelle he turns into Malcolm Bradbury.

Even Identity Crises

("US professor had 34 academic aliases" — *THES*).

Ah. Dr Droggett. Thanks so much for popping in. I just wanted to have a quite word with you about a little matter that's cropped up.
Only too pleased Professor Lapping. Nothing serious I hope.
No, not really, Droggett. Shouldn't take a moment.
Jolly good.
Now I'm certain there's a perfectly satisfactory explanation. Droggett, but I have to tell you that we've had a rather tricky letter this week from a prominent civic university in the north of England.
Sir?
And. . . well. . . quite frankly, Droggett, they've written to say that they believe that you may be working for them.
What's that sir?
They believe — and I must say that the large colour snap they enclose with their letter does lend some credibility to their argument — that you are a part-time lecturer employed by them under the name of Professor Linklater.
Linklater?
That's right, Droggett. Do you deny this charge?
Not exactly sir, no. But it is, as you say, only a part-time post and one which I find perfectly compatible with my other commitments.
Your other commitments at *this* university?
Yes. Those commitments. . . and a very small amount of other external part-time work.
For example?
Well, since you press me sir, I must admit that I'm lucky enough to be Professor Lionel Bonnington of Leicester University.
Oriental studies?
Exactly sir.
Anything else Droggett?
Dr Kurt Lobenstein.
Sheffield? Computer science?
Yes sir. It's more or less a straight run up the M1 from Leicester.
That's the lot?

Yes indeed. Apart that is, from a minor administrative role which is of a slightly delicate nature.

I think you can rely on my professional discretion in such matters. Droggett.

Well sir, and you'll understand why I'd prefer this to remain strictly between ourselves, I am also proud to be the present vice chancellor of. . .

Good heavens. Now I see the resemblance. It's just the moustache.

Exactly sir. So you'll appreciate the need. . .

Quite so.

Do you wish to take this whole business any further Professor Lapping?

No, not really, Droggett. I must admit there are no complaints about your work in this department. It seems well up to the standard which is required of a senior lecturer.

Thank you sir. So I may go?

Not so quickly Droggett. I don't think this mater can be completely swept under the carpet. In fact, in view of your special abilities in this direction I wish to impose a minor but appropriate sanction.

Sir?

Briefly Droggett, I wonder if you'd mind attending faculty board meetings for the rest of this term.

As punishment, sir?

No, Droggett. As me, *As me.*

And Other Pathologies

The doctor will see you now, Professor Lapping.

Thank you. Thank you.

Ah Lapping! Do take a seat. What seems to be the trouble?

I'm sorry to bother you at the Student Medical Centre. But it's the scripts!

The scripts?

It's no good, doctor. I can't mark them any more.

The examination scripts?

They're still there. Piled up on my desk. After six days.

Professor Lapping, do please relax. Now, tell me your symptoms. Any sign, for example, of the handwriting on these scripts seeming to spin before your eyes as you try to read it?

That's it. That's it. It positively wobbles from side to side. How did you know?

And have you found that sentences stop and start for no apparent reason and paragraphs go on for ever?

That's it exactly. You've met the condition before?

It's not unknown in medical circles. But it appears with varying degrees of intensity. May I ask — and I'd appreciate your frankness — if you ever find yourself turning over a page without any clear idea as to whether you've already read it?

Time and time again!

And are there occasions when after turning to a new page of script you have the overwhelming sense that you have read the new page already?

That as well!

And times when paradoxically you have the distinct sensation that you must have skipped a page because the new page appears to have no logical connection with the previous one?

The very feeling!

And is there any sign at all — the merest hint — of the onset of Heinz Syndrome?

Heinz Syndrome?

The recurrent sense that all the scripts you mark are of identical middle-ground quality and must therefore all receive the self-same mark of 57?

I can't shake it off.

Professor Lapping, you appear to have contracted what we doctors call Scriptic Neurosis. After many years in higher education — grading, examining — your evaluative sense simply atrophies. I advice cold baths, relaxation and a little less drinking. All right?

But what is the prognosis, doctor?

You'd like a frank medical assessment?

Yes, yes.

In that case, I have to say that on the present evidence I can't rate you any higher than a solid lower second.

Severe Frustration

"We are like silent screen actors. We have to publish. . . in journals that nobody reads" — Dr Steven Reicher of Exeter University addressing a British Psychological seminar on legitimacy in research (*THES,* April 22).

THE BRITISH JOURNAL OF UNREADABLE PSYCHOLOGY
VOL 59 NO. 3

From the Editor

A recent survey into the readership of this journal *(Braithwaite and Flummox, 1988a)* has revealed that statistically there is none. Although 99.4 of all academic psychologists who were interviewed declared that they "knew of the journal", and 98.73 regarded it as "an eminently respectable scientific publication", an average of only 0.0007 of the sample (or to be specific, Dr K.L.D. Mamsey of Nottingham University) had actually read anything but the contents page in the last 12.5 years.

Comparative work indicates that this is not an exclusive feature of academic journals in psychology. Finke and Grasshopper *(1988c)* in a seminal study demonstrated that a similar readership profile held true for a range of other journals including *The British Journal of Dull Empirical Facts about Political Science, The Comparative Journal of Long Marxist Articles,* and *the International Journal of Dubious Ideas About Fairly Well-Known Poems and Novels.*

Earlier studies of such journal non-readership have largely been confined to non-readers themselves. Gravitas and Golightly *(1974)* for example, found that 86 per cent of non-journal readers positively "felt much better" for not reading journals, and only 3.2 per cent experienced "mild anxiety or guilt", while Philippson and Snapdriver *(1981b)* found a small group of "pathological non-readers" (18 per cent of the academic population) who made a definite point of skirting library shelves on which such journals might be displayed.

In recent years, however, research interest in journal non-readership has also begun to take into account the effect of such behaviour on those who are responsible for the production of the unread journals. Klaxon, Devereux and Nancyboy *(1986b)* using a modified MPIE scale have established that "unread editors" are more liable than members of a control group of poorly-paid first year undergraduates to agree with the statement that "sometimes I feel my entire life has been an utter and complete waste of time" (p = 000.1). These low self-ratings were subsequently attributed by Fudlow and Trivett (1987) to what they called the "Unread Paradox". This asserts that the only way in which editors of unread journals (UJ) might reduce their current high level of frustration (HF) is bringing this frustration to the attention of their readers (AR) in the pages of the journal. But this possibility, is of course, blocked by the very absence of such readers in the first place.

In these circumstances the present editor of this journal feels it appropriate to adopt the stratagem recommended by Aloes and Silksmith *(1988b).* According to these researchers, attention may be drawn to written journal material which would normally remain unread through juxtaposing the message to be conveyed with a form of expression which immediately stands out as contextually dissonant. This, in their phrase, "re-directs the reader's attention to the preceding message". May I therefore take this opportunity to resign forthwith from my current editorial position and so SOD THE LOT OF YOU.

Deeply Personal Problems

Listen, darling.
Hmmmm.
Must be midnight.
Oh yes.
Happy *happy* New Year, darling.
Thank you very much.
You know, I did so enjoy tonight. Just the two of us for a change after all those legions of relatives over Christmas.
Mmmm.
Did you like it as much as I did, darling?
Well, as you say, it was certainly a change.
And then it was so lovely to come to bed early and listen to your new Mozart.
Oh yes.
I don't think I can remember a nicer end to an old year. So much better than going to one of those silly academic parties where all the radicals take ideological exception to the whole idea of celebrating the arrival of the New Year, and the rest of the faculty cross hands with their spouses and mumble half a verse of Auld Lang Syne. Tonight was really different, wasn't it?
No doubt about that.
And then there was. . . well. . you know.
What?
You know.
Oh yes. *That*.
How was it for you, darling?
Well, you know. It was. . . erm. . .
Was it just a little bit special?
I don't really have any particular comment to make.
None at all?
Not really.
You can't even bring yourself to say that it was good.
Erm. . .
Or at least better than average?
I'd rather not.
Darling, you know very well that I completely support the AUT stand on pay.
Yes, darling.
But do you really have to start your assessment boycott quite so soon?

Holidays Are Essential

Venezia, September 1.

Dear Maureen,
Venice is good as ever. The Tintorettos still astonish. And Ruskin still quite quite wrong about Veronese. Thought I saw good old Piercemüller inside St Marks yesterday but lost him in the Byzantine gloom. Weather glorious. Tourists frightful. *Plus ca change.*

One small thing. I only realized when we got to Milano that I'd completely forgotten to send out that letter to new First Years welcoming them to the department. Could you be a brick and knock out something along the usual lines: "We all look forward to meeting you in October — university is far less structured than school — don't expect too much too soon". And then a line about "all courses and tutors being subject to last minute modification without any warning whatsoever". That sort of thing. Anyway, see you soon.
Arrivederci
"Prof" Lapping.

Venezia, September 1

Dear Maureen,
Lovely old Venice. It never changes. The Bellinis at the Accademia still astonish. And how right Ruskin was about Giorgione. Thought I saw good old Piercemüller in St Marks Square yesterday but he seemed to disappear up the campanile. Pasta and vino splendid. Tourists dreadful. *C'est la vie.*

One small thing. I suddenly realized as we were coming out of Il Forza del Destino in Verona that I'd completely forgotten to fix up an office for our New Blood chappie. If something isn't done he'll turn up and have nowhere to go but the duplicating room. So could you be an angel and settle him down in B161. Just shove in a desk, half-a-dozen chairs, two bookcases, a filing cabinet and the usual blackboard. That sort of thing. Anyway, see you soon.
Arrivederci
Derek (Quintock)

Venezia, September 1

Dear Maureen,
Excuse handwriting but scribbling this on a Linea Una vaporetto bound for Lido. Venice as wonderful as ever. But fearfully crowded. Only some fast footwork in St Marks yesterday got me away from Lapping *and* Quintock!

One small thing. You remember the Spanish air controllers' business? Well, that rather set back our holiday and so it looks as though we'll be over here until near the end part of October (about November 3): This creates some slight difficulty for the first two of my Second Year lectures on Language and Thought and I was wondering if you could possibly be a sport and handle them for me. I usually start with "Which came first — Language or Thought?" — and then move on to the absurdities of both positions with a brief "mensh" of Whorf, Sapir and Chomsky on the way. But I leave the details to you. I'd really be *molto obligato!*

Must dash now and brush up my tan. The way I'm going you may not recognize me when I return!

Ciao for now
"Doc" Piercemüller.

CHAPTER FIVE

Vice-Chancellors and Chief Executives

At the very pinnacle of Britain's new institutions of higher education stand the lonely men (women need not apply) who must lead the way into the next millenium.

Even Vice-Chancellors Must Be Appraised

"As part of measuring performance, universities' vice-chancellors should be appraised" — Report in The THES of a paper by the Standing Conference of Arts and Social Sciences.

VICE CHANCELLORS ASSESSMENT QUESTIONNAIRE No.1

Time allowed: One hour.
Answer All Questions

1. An amendment in the Education Reform Bill proposes the abolition of the title "vice chancellor". Which of the following alternatives would you prefer?
a) Director
b) Managing Director
c) Witchfinder General

2. You are about to attend an important university meeting (e.g. senate, professional board, council). What "little get-togethers" will you arrange in the half-hour before?
a) A brisk chat with the registrar/bursar/pro vice chancellor
b) A quick nod and a wink to one or two compliant professors
c) A "watch it or you're next" meeting with any potential oppostion

3. What answer would an inquirer receive if they were to ask your secretary how many times in the last three years you had accepted the offer of a free trip abroad to talk about a subject not unrelated to the Present Strengths

and Future Prospects of the British University System?
a) Somewhere between 1 and 5
b) Rather more than 5
c) "I'm sorry but the vice chancellor is away on important business"

4. Does your portrait already hang in the administrative block? (If "yes" then go straight to Question 5. If "no" answer the following:)
When your portrait is commissioned which of the following formats would you feel to be most appropriate?
a) A modest photographic portrait
b) A head and shoulder water colour
c) A life-sized oil

5. Which of the following techniques have you favoured in your recent attempts to persuade departments in your university to accept major reductions in their resources?
a) Extended discussion and negotiation
b) Secret plots and coalitions
c) Veiled threats
d) Open blackmail
e) Hand-to-hand combat

6. When you look back to the "good old days" of the sixties and early seventies, which aspects of your work do you most miss?
a) Making new academic appointments
b) Ignoring letters from the UGC
c) Sending down radical students

7. Which of the following sentences are you able to use in public without a faint smile playing around your lips?
"This university is fully committed to the maintenance of a strong and vigorous department of:
a) Geology
b) Sociology
c) Philosophy

8. Which of the following would give you the greatest sense that you were doing a worthwhile job?
a) A vote of confidence from the local Association for University Teachers
b) A long letter of praise from Professor Sir Mark Richmond
c) The suggestion of a wink from Robert Jackson

And Forge New Alliances

AUT urges universities to withdraw funding from CVCP, *THES.*

The Athenaeum. Lunchtime.
I mean who do they think they are?
Beats me.
It's not as though most of them got their positions on merit.
Quite so. Quite so.
At least half of our lot were appointed to lectureships in the early 1970s when we were offering readerships to people who'd popped in to fix the central heating.
And aren't they selfish? Most of mine are quite incapable of seeing anything beyond their own department.
Or their own research.
Or their own promotion.
Quite unable to appreciate the skill it takes for us to run all those university committees.
To provide that important sense of democratic decision making.
While simultaneously doing precisely what the bursar tells us.
And most of them have so little political judgement. No proper notion of what a thoroughly nice chap Kenneth Baker can be when you really get to know him.
And their general appearance. So depressing. Not a smart suit or shirt between them.
Those scraggy beards in the English department.
The baggy corduroy in philosophy.
The squashed Hush Puppies in education.
Ugh.
And when you think what we do for them socially. All those receptions to make them feel they're loved.
The canapés and sherry.
The yards of small talk to their dull spouses.
Ingrates.
The only word.
It's funny really, but remember the end of the Sixties?
You mean the occupations and the arson and the gates being broken down and the nude sunbathing and the Queen being offered that bottle of wine?
That's it. Well, I never thought I'd hear myself saying it, but you know when it comes to present day universities — give me the students every time.
Right on.

New Coalitions

University vice chancellors are to send out letters to all parents of students setting out the threat to university autonomy contained in the Education Reform Bill — THES.

The Vice-Chancellor's Office, Friday 29th January 1988

Dear Mrs Jolyon,

I do hope that your son/daughter. . . **HELEN**. . . is still enjoying his/her time at our university. I must say that we love having him/her with us and the. . . **PHILOSOPHY**. . . department tell me that he/she is now making good/fairly good/quite good/progress.

You'll no doubt be surprised to receive a letter from a "Vice-Chancellor". In the normal run of things we don't have much to do with parents except on degree day, and even then I must admit we're rather difficult to spot behind all the robes and the ceremonial mace! But you'll find a "Vice-Chancellor" at most British universities, beavering away behind the scenes, making these small but crucial decisions which ensure that our universities maintain their international reputation: closing down the odd department, sending out the occasional premature retirement notice.

Now a few years ago we decided it would be a jolly good idea if all the vice-chancellors in the country got together and had an organization of their own. We called our little get-together the CVCP and we had a simply splendid time chatting to each other over a few drinks and keeping up a hectic round of social activities. Occasionally, we even managed to issue a document about university education but as we were largely an unelected group of amiable old buffers no-one took all that much notice.

All that rather changed when the Conversatives came into office. Right from the start all their people were thoroughly nice to us. Even the ministers seemed to enjoy nothing so much as coming over for a drink and a game of croquet on the lawn behind our beautiful offices in WC1. It's true that sometimes they did cheat a little but we were on the whole happy to let them win because they so obviously enjoyed our company.

I'm now writing to your because of what's happened in the last couple of months. Much as in the past we'd been playing along quite happily with the new minister — letting him move the occasional hoop and have one or two free shots. But we've now learnt to our utter amazement that he won't be coming to see us any more. He says he's got other friends called "businessmen" and anyway he never liked us much in the first place. Quite honestly, it's all most upsetting, and so I wonder if you would be good enough to sign the letter below and post if off to him as soon as possible. Thanking you in anticipation.

The Vice-Chancellor

Cut here

....

Dear Mr Baker
Please would you let the vice-chancellors have their ball back.
Thank you.

(Parent) ....

They Must Control Student Numbers With Precision

I'm sorry, Vice Chancellor, but I really must object in the strongest terms. Are you seriously proposing that the Department of Theoretical Accountancy be given an extra quota place on the sole grounds that its A level average score has risen to 11.75?

That is indeed the proposal, Professor Greet.

Well then, sir, I would feel that it was only natural justice to accord identical treatment to my own Department of Mechanical Ethics. And I speak, sir, not as a member of that department, but as an objective observer.

But Professor Greet, surely the A level average in your own department is 11.25; that is, exactly 0.5 below the Department of Theoretical Accountancy. By any calculation that must place you at a disadvantage.

Not at all, sir. Your calculations have failed to include the necessary statistical correction for mature students. It is agreed university policy that their A level scores should not affect the overall average. And, in fact, one of our admissions this year was just such a mature student with only two E grade scores. If he is removed our average rises to 11.75.

I'm sorry Professor Greet, but as you will see if you inspect the Admissions Report, those allowances have already been made in the penultimate column and would appear to give you an overall average of 11.5 and not as you say, 11.75. In any case, when similar adjustments are made for the Department of Theoretical Accountancy, they produce a figure of 11.88, which is, even by your own figure of 11.75, still a clear 0.13 ahead.

Vice Chancellor?

Yes, Professor Ternbite.

I wonder, sir, if such an important matter as the quota for individual departments should be decided by a mere mathematical fraction. After all, sir, the 0.13 you mention, is no more than, say, one thirtieth of a B grade at A level. Might I, by way of contrast — and here I am, incidentally, using my own Department of Applied Metaphysics as an example, so you may think it appropriate for me to leave the room when the eventual vote is taken — but by way of contrast, may I point out that the median, as distinct from the mean of our department's A level scores is in fact, 12. This is an increase of 0.5 — one whole half, sir — on last year's score. It would seem to me to be an almost unanswerable case for a quota improvement.

I certainly see the strength of the argument, Professor Ternbite, but unfortunately it does have to be set against the 0.07 decline in your ratio of applications to places, together with a percentage decline of 0.00073 in the number of candidates actually placing your department first in their UCCA choices.

Well, Vice Chancellor, this seems to be an impasse. How do you suggest we proceed?

Oh, in the usual way I think, gentlemen. In the face of such statistical imponderables, it is surely most judicious to return to trusted principles.

You mean, first publish ten pages of statistical detail. . .

Exactly, Professor Greet, and then take five places off the social sciences and distribute them around members of this committee.

Respond Rationally To The UGC

I don't suppose you'd like to hold it for a moment, registrar?

Well, thank you, vice chancellor. Just for a second if I may.

There.

Thank you. *Isn't it beautiful.* So compact, and yet so full of meaning.

The final, final, final version.

Just 24 hours before the deadline.

D'you remember those grey days back in February, when it all seemed impossible.

Who could forget them, vice chancellor. Sixty-three totally contradictory responses from every department and sub-department in the university.

Forty-seven subcommittees.

One hundred and twenty two drafts.

Ninety-four references back.

Five hundred and forty photocopies of the original UGC letter.

The nine-hour debate on senate before the vote to exclude the word "Judas" from our answer to the question on the recent role of the UGC.

But then there were the lighter moments, vice chancellor.

Indeed, indeed.

The political science department insisting upon that reference to the Owl of Minerva.

And catering committee misreading that reference to sandwich courses.

Yes, yes. and sorting out the split infinitives in the AUT response.

And Professor Dogberry going berserk at faculty board over tenure.

Oh yes. Unforgettable. "Tenure is inviolable. Tenure is inviolable." Banging the table with his shoe.

Punching the deputy bursar.

Oh yes. And dear old Professor Emwort jogging around outside the council chamber with that *"Who's too old at 60?"* placard on her chest.

Memories. Memories.

And the whole enterprise crowned, if I may say so, vice chancellor, by your final paragraph.

You mean the bit about, "all in all, taking every special interest into account, ignoring any view which might be remotely radical, looking at the matter with resolute objectivity, but not being afraid to face the future and recognize the importance of electronics, it is the firm belief of this university that things should stay exactly as they are".

Marvellous.

Thank you.

Well, into the envelope it goes.

Erm. . . registrar. Just before you seal it.

Sir?

Pop in this £10 note, will you? One never knows.

Quite so, sir.

Rationally _And_ Objectively

I wonder if we might now turn to Question Number 3 in the UGC letter. That's the first paragraph on Page Four.

I'm sorry, vice chancellor, what page did you say?

That's perfectly all right, Professor Dreyfus. It *is* a large number of questions. This particular question — Question 3 — is on page four.

Page *four*, vice chancellor?

That's it, Doctor Kernitz. But let me read it aloud so that there can be no chance of confusion.

Excuse me, vice chancellor.

Yes, Doctor Comstock?

I wondered, sir, and I only raise this because I believe there might be others around the table who share my opinion, but I wonder if it would be at all helpful if you were to read the question aloud.

Thank you, Doctor Comstock, I'm most grateful for your timely intervention. Well, Question 3 reads: *"Should a significant number of institutions be closed between 1900 and 1994, and, if so, what criteria and what machinery should decide which"*. So this — as I read it — is a perfectly straightforward question about whether we think a significant number of universities should be closed between 1990 and 1994 — and if so — why. Yes, Professor Swinefleet, would you like to get us started on this one?

Certainly, sir. With reference to the first part of the question, may I propose *three*. Three universities for closure.

Thank you, Professor Swinefleet. A modest and helpful proposal. Is there a seconder? Yes, thank you, Doctor Comstock. Well, that seems to meet with general agreement. *Three* it is. Now may we be a little more specific. Which particular institutions would seem to us to be best suited for this course of action? Professor Blandish?

May I propose Leicester, sir?
Seconded.

Good. This is most constructive. Any other suggestions? Yes, Doctor Kernitz?

Erm. Manchester, sir.
Seconded.
And erm. . . and erm. . . Huddersfield.

Well, Doctor Kernitz, I think perhaps your enthusiasm is running away with you there. . .

Erm, *Halifax*, sir. . . no, no. . . erm. . . *Hull*. That's it. *Hull*.
Seconded.

Fine. That's Leicester, Manchester and Hull for closure. Any other nominations? Jolly good. Can I see those in favour? Virtually *unanimous*. Now may we turn to the *second* part of this question and delineate the exact criteria which lie behind our choice. And, of course, here we need to concentrate upon what one might call matters of general principle. Can anyone offer me a form of words? Yes, Professor Teetlebaum?

Well, sir, I was thinking of something on the following lines: *"Anywhere at all. . . erm"*.

Yes, please go on, Professor Teetlebaum. This already sounds most promising.

Well, sir, how about: *"Anywhere at all. . . so long as it's not us"*.

That'll do nicely.

And Be Prepared to Change Direction When Reason Demands

"Vice chancellors welcome the Government's announcement of a rise in tuition fees" — THES.

Vice Chancellor. Professor Lapping is here to see you.

Excellent. Gordon! There you are! My dear old chap. Good heavens, don't stand on ceremony. Come in. Come in. So nice of you to spare the time for a little chat. My word, you're looking well!

Really?

Positively blooming. Lots of life in the old dog yet, eh?

One hopes·so.

Yes indeed. Now Gordon, down to business. As you know, over the past five years we've been implementing a carefully considered, exhaustively researched, academic plan within this university — the plan we entitled *Capitalizing on our Academic Strengths.* You'll probably have been aware of how the actual details of that master plan have affected the day-to-day working of your own department of culture and media studies.

You mean the way in which it reduced our quota of undergraduate students by just over 30 per cent?

That's more or less right.

And then used our resulting favourable staff-student ratio as a reason for refusing any replacement appointments in the department so that in the past five years our staff numbers have fallen from eight to three?

That's the sort of thing.

And then systematically taken away our rooms and offices and allocated them to computer studies, accountancy and business studies?

That's certainly one aspect of the picture.

And then drastically reduced our departmental budget and secretarial allowance on the grounds that we were only average in the UGC rankings and lacked massive research funding?

That on the whole has been the gist of the overall plan.

And meanwhile totally ignored admission statistics which showed that we were one of the departments in the university with an ever increasing number of undergraduate applications?

Could hardly have put it better myself, Gordon. A very adequate summary. But let me be the first to tell you that that is now all in the past.

All in the past?

Oh yes. From now there'll be no more cutbacks in your department. Oh no. From now on you can regard your three staff, half a secretary, four rooms, and shared duplicator, as permanent resources.

Really?

And what's more, just to keep them all company, next October we'll be sending you one hundred extra first year undergraduates. Yes Gordon, it's all part of our brand new, carefully considered, exhaustively researched, five-year plan — *To Hell with Academic Strengths: Pack the Buggers In.* Now, can I tempt you to a Tio Pépé.

And Justify That Change

Any other business? Yes, Doctor Sproat?

Vice chancellor, I hope you will not in any way construe this as an example of special pleading, but I wonder if you have had time to consider the implications for your present academic plan of the UGC's review of philosophy — a review, which, I understand, recommends the strengthening of 16 departments with additional staff, departments among which is numbered my own.

I see no problem there at all, Doctor Sproat.

No problem?

None whatsoever. On the basis of a preliminary reading I would say that the thinking in the review is very much in line with our own ideas about the unique importance which we attach to the study of philosophy within this university.

But vice chancellor, I see in paragraph 22/4/B of the academic plan for the next five years — and you'll excuse me if I quote directly — "We regard philosophy as essentially marginal when set alongside our central academic commitments to accountancy, electronic engineering and hotel management. That hardly makes it sound _uniquely_ importantly".

Really, Doctor Sproat. You must not be quite so literal. I should have thought it obvious that in that context the word "marginal" clearly does not mean unimportant — it rather seeks to convey the sense of a discipline which runs alongside the margin of all our thinking — which provides, as it were, constant annotations, to our conventional ideas, a vital commentary upon all aspects of academic work.

I see. But when Doctor Tomkins raised this question at faculty board two months ago. . .

Doctor Tomkins?

My colleague. The other member of my department.

He's still with us?

Yes indeed. And when he raised the question of the treatment of philosophy in the academic plan you told him — minute 43/89 — that your personal knowledge of philosophy had led you to believe that it was "largely a self-indulgent exercise which would never in a million years meet the Chilver standard of relevance".

Would never _meet,_ Doctor Sproat. Would never exactly _meet._ For the simple reason that it went above and beyond it. Transcended the standard of relevance.

So you feel that Doctor Tomkins and I might now with confidence apply for additional staff?

Not exactly additional, Doctor Sproat. But we do have a chap with some spare time in accountancy who could pop over. . .

Thank you, vice chancellor. And perhaps you yourself, with your own

philosophical background might lend a hand from time to time? Well I. . .

Because Doctor Tomkins and I have already taken the liberty of pencilling you in for the third year option in advanced sophistry.

They Must Find Time To Listen

A new Report by Professor Sizer on rationalization in universities spells out the necessity of allowing "argument, debate and controversy during implementation of cuts" — THES.

Yes, Doctor Tremlett. I detect a slight movement in your right hand. A comment on the new university plan, perhaps?

Well, yes, Vice Chancellor. I apologise for taking up this Committee's time, but I wonder if an objective outsider might not feel that your proposal for my own department. . .

Yes, do go on, Doctor Tremlett. We're anxious to hear your views.

Well, I wonder if such an objective outsider might not find your proposals somewhat unreasonable.

In what sense, Doctor Tremlett?

In the sense that you say we must bear more than our fair share of the proposed cuts in that we are only a small department and therefore lacking in viability.

Press on, Doctor Tremlett. *Argument, debate, controversy.* That's what we want.

Well, it has to be said, Sir, that we are only a small department in the first place, because over the last five years you have systematically reduced our quota of undergraduates.

That's more like it. Doctor Tremlett. Press your point. Press it home.

And you've then quite illogically — one might say, perversely — used our lack of undergraduates as a reason for not replacing members of staff and refusing to appoint a new professorial head of department.

But what about the way in which we've planned the present round cuts? Surely there's some room for argument there as well.

Oh yes indeed. That was verging on the outrageous. You blatantly aligned yourself with the interests of the large and powerful departments — with economics, electronics law. . .

Yes. Yes.

. . . And quite inexcusably promoted the interests of such fundamentally non-academic subjects as accountancy and computing in a crude attempt to ingratiate yourself and the university with the UGC.

Splendid stuff. Doctor Tremlett. Just what the Professor ordered.

I tell you this, Vice Chancellor, I do not speak only for myself in this.

95

Oh no! There are others around this table who are equally anxious for the chance to talk as I am doing — to re-affirm their commitment ot the idea of a university as a community of scholars.

More debate! More argument! More controversy! An excellent idea. Yes indeed. So may I turn without delay to the date of the next meeting. In line with the recommendations of the Jarratt Report on university committees — another absolutely first-class report, I must say — this will be held on February 27, 1991. Quite honestly. I'm rather looking forward to it. Now is there Any Other Business?

To Reward Appropriately

Mr Pelling is here to see you, Vice Chancellor.

Pelling? Pelling?

Promotions, Vice Chancellor.

Ah yes. Thank you, Mrs Matthews. Do send him in.

This way, Mr Pelling.

Ah Pelling. There you are. Good to see you.

Thank you, Vice Chancellor.

How are things in the old department of philosophy.

Oh, you know, ticking over. Of course, we're desperately short. . .

Excellent. Pelling?

Vice Chancellor?

Pelling, how long have we known each other?

I don't think I've ever met you before, Vice Chancellor.

Not *personally,* **Pelling. As colleagues, Working alongside each other in the same university?**

Oh, about 14 years.

That's right. About 14. And during that time you've been conscientiously labouring away in the department of philosophy. A true servant of the university.

One does one's. . .

And that's why I'm pleased to be able to tell you that your application to the Promotions Committee this year was considered very seriously indeed.

Well, I didn't feel I had too much of a chance. But as everybody else. . .

Pelling, let me be completely frank. There were things against you. On paper your research work does look somewhat modest. Only the one article in the *British Journal of Applied Ontology* **during the last decade. But it was a good article, Pelling. A solid, non-nonsense, middle-ground traditional, article.**

Thank you, Vice Chancellor.

And although your head of department was rather less than flattering about one aspect of your teaching — what was the phrase — ah yes — "About

as inspiring as a lump of used lard'', there seems no doubt at all about your ability to take the register and arrive more or less on time for both lectures and seminars.

Thank you, Vice Chancellor.

And there was, of course, additional evidence on the administrative side. It's not every Departmental First Aid Officer who can boast that there has been only one major fatality among staff during their period of incumbency.

Thank you, Vice Chancellor.

So I'm delighted to tell you that, all in all, looking at the rounded picture, the committee decided, after considerable discussion, that your promotion be recommended.

Really?

Yes indeed. And that only leaves us with the formalities. If you'd sign here and here, I can go ahead and report your promotion and new status to council at their next meeting.

New status, Vice Chancellor?

Untenured, Pelling. Got you at last. *You're fired.*

Maintain Confidentiality

An independent report on Aberdeen University has criticized the secretive manner in which the university is run. THES.

Vice chancellor, the registrar is here.

Not so loud, Mrs Enderby. Not so loud. Ah, Charles. There you are. Do come in.

Thank you vice chancellor. I understand the pro-vice chancellor is on his way up the fire escape.

Excellent. Ah yes, I see him at the window now. There. Quietly does it, Gerald.

Thank you vice chancellor. Hello, Charles.

Hello Gerald. Did Mary enjoy the Mozart?

Very much, thank you. So kind of you to get the tickets.

Think nothing of it.

And thank you, vice chancellor for the excellent champagne.

A great pleasure, Gerald. The least one can do on the birthday of the pro-vice chancellor's wife.

She was most gratified. Said you must pop round soon for some of your favourite chocolate cake.

Scrumptious. Now, is everybody comfortable. Good, well, the first item on the agenda today is. . . registrar, is that door locked?

I'll check it, sir. Yes indeed. Quite, quite secure.

Good. And can you can all hear me if I s-p-e-a-k l-i-k-e t-h-i-s?
Yes, sir.
Excellent. Now, the first item is the department of culture and media studies. My own feeling — shhhhh — is that someone outside the door?
I think not, sir.
Can't be too careful. Walls have ears, you know. My own feeling is that we must consider very carefully the status of the department both in terms of its national standing and its importance within the development plans of this university, and then, and only then, c-l-o-s-e i-t d-o-w-n.
So we'll proceed in the usual way?
Not quite so loud, Gerald. Yes, I'll propose a small independent departmental review committee at Senate this Friday. And that'll mean you, Charles, as secretary, myself as chairman, and the pro-vice chancellor as vice chairman. And I see the recommendation for closure coming out about mid-August when all the AUT Trots are on their backs in Tuscany.
Sounds perfect.
Good. That's settled then. Now perhaps we could move on to the next few tasks on today's agenda. In no particular order I've got the university's submission to the UGC, abolition of the history and philosophy departments, contracting out library services, sacking the resident artist, taking back degrees from students who participate in demonstrations, and changing my name to emperor.
Vice-chancellor. . .
Piano, Charles, piano.
I'm sorry, vice chancellor. But I wonder if we might have a little breather before we move on further.
Good heavens, Charles. Tired all ready?
Not really, sir. It's just that with three of us it does get a trifle hot inside this cupboard.

Preside Over Essential Committees

Tuesday Afternoon Time Immemorial Committee
Minutes of the meeting held on 11th January 1989.
Present: The Vice-Chancellor (Chair), Doctor Q.A Spermhandler, Doctor D.T.W. Wratchet, Mr L.S. Horsefountain.
Also present: J.W. Brooding, L.A. Catchment.
In attendance: Miss I.J. Punting (Secretary).
Popped in for a moment: T.H. Local.
Apologies received from Professor C. C. Gauntlet.

89/1 Approval of the Minutes of the Meeting held on 13th December 1988
It was noted that the name of Professor Dingbat appeared in the list of

apologies for the last meeting of this committee. After some discussion it was agreed that as Professor Dingbat was not in fact a member of this committee or indeed, as far as anyone knew, of the university itself, 'Apology for Absence' should be deleted from the minutes.

89/2 Matters Arising from the Minutes

a) Doctor Spermhandler reported that since the last meeting he had been looking into one or two questions raised by minute 88/126 but so far did not have any of the answers. After a detailed discussion it was agreed that no further action would be taken on any of these matters until after the committee had had the opportunity to hear further from Doctor Spermhandler.

89/3 Jarratt Recommendations

Doctor D.T.W. Wratchet explained to members of the committee that they would shortly be receiving a preliminary copy of his subcommittee's deliberations on a proposal from the Outside Speakers' Committee that the Jarratt recommendations on streamlining decision-making in university committees be declared "inappropriate" for those committees which had within the last 10 years not made anything which would be recognized by any reasonable person as a decision. Doctor Q.R. Spermhandler thanked Dr. D.T.W. Wratchet for the diligence he had displayed in detecting the imminent arrival of a report from his own subcommittee.

89/4 The Vice-Chancellor

Following the departure of the student represntatives, Mr L.S. Horsefountain raised the whole question of the Vice-Chancellor.

89/5 Any Other Business

Mr T.H. Local asked for permission to point out to the committee that once again 'Any Other Business' had been confined to the end of the agenda, a position which ensured that any business raised under the heading would be likely to receive somewhat more cursory treatment than that traditionally accorded to business appearing at an earlier stage. After a detailed discussion it was agreed by 4 to 3 (with 2 abstentions) that for a trial period of six years, 'Any Other Business' would now appear at the head of the committe's agenda, immediately· before 'Apologies for absence'.

89/6 Death of Doctor Q.A. Spermhandler

Miss I.J. Punting (Secretary) asked for permission through the chair to note that Doctor Spermhandler had expired sometime during the second half of the present committee meeting. As it was now 5 o'clock it was agreed without division that this item would be placed on the agenda for the next meeting.

And Pioneer New Directions

. . . Perhaps we might now move on to item 34 on the agenda **Mature and Part-time Students: New Initiatives.** You have before you a lengthy but, in my opinion, remarkably concise paper, which is the result of many months of painstaking work by Professor Dingbat and the other dedicated members of his sub-committee. Before we move to a general discussion I wonder if I might ask Professor Dingbat if he'd be so good as to speak to his document.

Yes indeed, Vice Chancellor. Might I first of all make absolutely sure that everybody around this table has a copy of the report.

I don't in any way want to hold up the proceedings, Vice Chancellor, particularly as this is obviously a matter of considerable importance for the future of this university, but I can't in all honesty say that I seem to have one.

I think you'll find it to your left, Doctor Wurlitzer. No — *left.* A little further. *That's it.*

Ah yes. I have it now.

Well, if I might briefly run over some of the ideas behind our thinking. You'll see that in the first part — that's pages eight to 36 — we have rehearsed the principal philosophical arguments about the nature of the university in contemporary society: a largely uncontentious section I would have thought, although you'll see that one of our number, Doctor Blagdon of History, has entered a minority opinion in which he questions our somewhat uncritical treatment of Rousseau.

Hear, hear.

We then move on to more substantive educational questions, and tackle the thorny and perennial issue of the maintenance of academic standards in a changing world. That's pages 42 to 85.

Hear, hear.

And then, after some brief reflections on education as essentially a process which extends throughout life rather than being confined to the formative years — that's pages 89 to 115 — we come to the final summary. I think it might be helpful, Professor Dingbat, if you were to read out the last paragraph of that summary. It does seem to capture the essential spirit of the document and also point to the way forward.

Hear, hear.

Thank you, Vice Chancellor. What we say is this — page 132, para 19 — "Quite frankly, we don't want any more mature or part-time students in this university, but as there's no one else around it looks as if we'll have to take them for the moment, even if many of them have got lousy A levels and one or two are downright bolshie but no matter what happens we're damned if we're going to do any evening teaching".

Thank you so much, Professor Dingbat. Now are there any interminable questions which could fruitlessly occupy us for another hour or so. Yes, Doctor Wurlitzer, I see that both your hands are raised.

CHAPTER SIX

Marketing the New University

It is no longer enough for the university or polytechnic to sit back and wait for their students to arrive. Nowadays students are customers and must be courted with all the assiduity which has traditionally been brought to bear upon such other commodities as life insurance and biscuits.

Old Property Must Go

"Ivory Towers Are Up For Sale" — **Professor Sir Mark Richmond, the new chairman of the Committee of Vice Chancellors and Principals.**

Joseph & Baker

Estate Agents Established 1979

IVORY TOWERS

We are pleased to announce the sale of this valuable historic property at a price which reflects its somewhat dilapidated current state (might well suit a DIY enthusiast). Among the outstanding features of this distinctively British Estate are the following:

The Well of Pure Knowledge

Up until a decade ago it was still possible to find residents drinking at this well but present purchasers are warned that it is now seriously contaminated by expedient research and a debilitating trickle of commercial sponsorship. (A similar deterioration may be noted in the adjoining *Fount of Inspiration*).

The Temple of Philosophy

A once splendid edifice which is now much reduced in size. Individual pillars are still standing but often in clumps of not more than two or three, and in many cases no attempt has been made to replace those cornices which have crumbled through old age (or early retirement).

101

The Bastion of Academic Integrity
This important part of the original estate benefits from several hundred years of careful and often heroic consolidation but has recently been mortgaged for the sake of a quiet life and is now in need of considerable renovation. (Parts of the building are only held together by hastily constructed rationalizations.)

The Groves of Academe
At one time these famous groves served to insulate the property from the clamour of outside interests but they are now decidedly threadbare following the partial refurbishment of the site as a *Park of Science*.

The Haven of Humanities
This large building is still a central element within the Ivory Towers estate, but serious subsidence is now affecting many of its original Middle English and Ancient Historical features.

The Path of Academic Merit
A narrow pathway which formerly led to the high ground of Ivory Towers but which is now grown over and may only be followed as far as the The Bar.

The Ancient Shrine of Education for Citizenship
Closed.

Price. 40 Pieces of Silver (or nearest offer)

Existing Products Be Re-Named

(Today — May 6 — the Social Science Research Council discusses proposals for a change of name)

Gentlemen, I wonder if you'd be good enough to raise your hands again? I think that last vote was close enough to merit a recount.

Excuse me, chairman, I'm afraid I'm just a little confused.

What's that, Charles?

Well, sir, are we still considering *Social Studies Research Council* **or is that one rejected?**

No, no. It's still *Social Studies Research Council.* You recall the list of advantages. In particular, the retention of the initials, with 'studies' simply replacing 'science'.

Jolly good. It's just that I don't recall us voting on the suggestion before this one.

Which one exactly do you mean, Charles?

The *Council for Economic Social and Related Studies,* **CESRS. Did we take a vote on that one?**

Yes, indeed. That was the vote before the last. Twelve to three against, if I recall correctly.

Ah, well, that's where the problem is. You see I rather thought we were twelve to three against an entirely different proposal.

Good heavens, Charles. Which one was that?

The ESRC. *The Economic and Social Research Council.* **Not the** *Council for Economic Social and Related Studies.*

Not at all. That was a very clear fourteen to one against.

Ah.

Of course, you could be getting confused with SPERC. That was the proposal immediately before ESRC.

SPERC, sir? I'm sorry. Could you just refresh my memory on that one?

Certainly, Charles, SPERC is the *Social, Psychological and Economic Research Council.*

Ah.

Which we threw out eleven to four, mainly on the grounds that things were bad enough already without the psychologists sticking their oar in. That all right now, Charles?

Yes, thank you, sir. My apologies.

Perfectly all right, Charles. Nothing simple about this matter. That's why they pay grown men like ourselves to sit around all day discussing it. Well now, let's move on to that recount. May I see hands raised? Thank you. That looks like nine to six against *Social Studies Research Council.*

Which means, chairman, that we've now rejected all the proposals submitted by the associations and organizations we've canvassed for the last three months?

Quite so, Charles. So it's a straight-forward case of falling back upon the compromise which was agreed with Sir Keith before this meeting.

You mean . . .

Exactly. This council will from now on be known as the *Social Marmalade Research Council.* Now can we move on to item four on the agenda — the proposal from the minister that all future meetings of this renamed council should take place under water. Could I see those in favour?

Departments And Universities Consumer Tested By The UGC

Well, thank you so much for all turning up this afternoon for our final meeting, especially when most of you must even now be making preparations for the annual vacation — a vacation, which, I must say, is richly deserved after all your recent hard labour on the research strengths of every university department in the country. *A magnificent achievement.* However, before we all depart to sunnier climes — Tuscany again for you Charles? *lucky fellow*

— there are one or two minor complaints about the rankings which need to be cleared up.

Sour grapes if you ask me.

In general, yes, George. But in a couple of cases — no more than 13 by the latest count — there does seem to have been some genuine grounds for misunderstanding. I've dealt with most of these on your behalf but I'd like to have your retrospective approval. There were *four* major departments, for example, which we hadn't mentioned at all in our lists and they rather wondered why not. I've remedied this by giving each of them an "average" and pointing out that it was purely a result of a *"clerical misunderstanding"*.

Excellent.

Then there are the *three* departments to which we gave "outstanding" rankings but which don't in fact exist. What I've done here is to write to the respective vice chancellors and apologise for the *"clerical oversight"*.

Excellent.

And then there are the *six* departments which we ranked as "below average" where their publication records as well as their total of research money places them well above most other departments in their disciplines. Here again, I felt some re-consideration was called for, so I've raised two of them to "average" and referred straightforwardly to our *"clerical mistake"*.

Excellent.

And then, finally, the most recent problem: the 45 odd professors of politics who have written in saying that the rankings of their discipline are most peculiar in that they include hardly any awards of "above average" or "outstanding". A bit tricky this one. But if the committees are prepared to agree then I thought we might award a couple of extra "outstandings" — perhaps to the leading signatories — and say that they were omitted from the orginal letter because of *"clerical error"*.

Excellent.

So that's that then. Let me once again wish all of you a splendid vacation. We'll meet again in the autumn, except, that is, for the special sub-committee which has a few final secret things to sew up with the DES.

Just one small point. Something for a future agenda no doubt.

Yes Charles?

How is it, I wonder, that we are saddled with such a desperately incompetent clerical staff?

Beats me, Charles. *Completely beats me.*

Public Relations Is Embraced

It is time to sharpen up your public relations: at the same time you must not frighten your academic colleagues by the bold headlines, the news flashes and the bright glossy approach — **from a British Council advertisement inviting university administrative staff to participate in a course on "Public Relations in Higher Education"** *(THES).*

NEW P.R. FEAR SWEEPS BRITAIN'S CAMPUSES

Don Takes Refuge

Doctor T.R.S. Waterspiegel (52) who has been missing from the Psychology Department for nearly seven weeks was last night found alive and relatively well in an oak wardrobe at his wife's mother's house. He claimed that he retreated to this temporary *asile* only after reading a university Public Relations handout on his ESRC research award for the study of concept formation in rodents. This was boldly headlined, "CASH BONANZA FOR LOCAL RATMAN". Doctor Waterspiegel's present condition is described as "persistently reclusive".

Struck Dumb

According to usually reliable sources, the Head of the Department of Social Institutions, Doctor G.R.Q. Salmonweather (52), has entirely lost the gift of speech, or indeed the capacity to make any meaningful sound whatsoever, since reading a university PR newsflash which described his department as "excellently equipped and containing some of the finest minds in the country". Doctor Salmonweather's department is at present housed in a bicycle shed and he is currently its sole member of staff.

Shaking All Over

A diagnosis of "galloping neuralgia" has been made in the unfortunate case of Doctor D.P.B. Bannistrader (52) who was overcome by a convulsive fit in the middle of Marks and Spencer's pyjama department last Wednesday. At the time Doctor Bannistrader was clutching in his teeth a copy of a glossy university P.R. handout advertising his new course on Internal Microscopy under the headline: "Internal Microscopy Refreshes the Parts Other Disciplines Cannot Reach".

Goodbye Mr Chips (nearly)

The showing of the new university PR video — "Come On Over To Our Place" — was temporarily interrupted last night when Doctor T.C.L. Senegalstone (52) collapsed during a sequence featuring the Academic Overture in which happy undergraduates were shown selecting essential texts from the university library. A colleague who helped to carry the don from the viewing room said that the look on his face could only be described as "horrified incredulity".

Killed by 'new' V.C.

"Death from misadventure" was the verdict in yesterday's enquiry into the sudden death from heart failure of Professor F.B.R. Topefaster (52). It was reported during the hearing that Professor Topefaster had been away from the university on a one year leave of absence and was therefore quite unprepared for the discovery at Faculty Board that the Vice Chancellor had been fitted out by the PR department with a bright new set of teeth, a glossy auburn wig, and a CVCP T-shirt bearing the legend VICE CHANCELLORS DO IT LYING DOWN.

Conferences Are High On The Agenda

Professor Lapping, are we, I wonder in some danger of being a shade pedantic?

Possibly, Doctor Quintock. Possibly.

All this argument over how much we could save by reducing the relative number of chocolate digestives and custard creams.

You have a proposal which will move us forward, Doctor Quintock?

Well, why not abolish afternoon biscuits altogether.

Abolish afternoon biscuits!

Why not? In these health conscious days it's difficult to imagine anyone complaining about their absence, and according to my quick calculations, such a move would save us nearly 20p per delegate — that's 150 by 20 — a full £30. At a stroke! Nearly three times the savings which would accrue from your proposed draconian cuts in the proportion of digestives and custard creams.

A Daniel come to judgment! Eureka!

Thank you, Doctor Quintock. I think I sense some general enthusiasm for your radical proposal. May we then move on to calculate the overall balance sheet for the conference.

Excuse me, Professor Lapping, I'm sorry I was rather late — last minute Easter shopping for the nippers — but I wonder . . .

Docter Piercemüller, might I ask you to reserve your comments until we've completed the final accounts? Thank you. Now, if we leave in the cost of afternoon biscuits without providing them — the Quintock amendment — and add that to the savings we've made by allocating one instead of two cartons of UHT milk to each bedroom, and by cutting out the option of Alpen at breakfast time, and by decreasing the size of the dinner plates so that we can get away with smaller portions of meat, then we seem to be left with an overall university cost per delegate of £73 for the two days of the conference — a total which when set against our proposed conference fee per delegate of £85 gives a net profit of £12 multiplied by 150 which — wait for it — means that there will be approximately £1,800 profit for the departmental

coffers.
Nice one!
Let's go for it!
Excuse me, Professor Lapping, but ...
Ah, Doctor Piercemüller, I nearly forgot you in the general excitement. What's your problem?
Well, Professor Lapping, as I said, I'm sorry I arrived rather late for this meeting, but I wonder ...
Yes?
I wonder if I might ask at this late stage about the nature of our proposed conference.
Its nature?
Its general topic — overall theme — subject matter.
Good heavens, Doctor Piercemüller. Don't try and rush us off our feet. First things first, eh?

With Full Co-Operation From Academic Staff

Professor Lapping?
Speaking.
Ah good. Fitch here. From the university's Accommodation, Vacation, and Conference Centre.
And what can I do for you, Mr. Fitch?
Well, Professor Lapping, you may remember that during last year's summer conference season you were kind enough to allow us to use your office for some overflow seminars involving members of NAPS — the National Association of Property Speculators.
Only too happy to help out in an emergency.
Excellent. Because we do rather seem to have another one on our hands this Easter. From Friday in fact. Immediately after your last tutorial of term.
More conference seminars?
Not exactly. More holiday trade. The coming thing you know. In fact it's our brand new 4-Day 18-32 Campus Carousel Break which is causing the trouble. A little over booked. So we were thinking of adapting your room. Nothing too structural you understand. But it would mean goodbye to books, filing cabinets, stacka chairs, anglepoise lamp, and that large portrait
You mean Roland Barthes, the distinguished French ...
Professor Lapping, let me be quite frank with you. Even if it were *Lionel* Bart it would have to go. It just doesn't fit in with our advertised ambience.
Ambience?
That's right. And I think you'll be pleasantly surprised at the transformation. A little discreet lighting, a few low tables, the deputy bursar stationed behind your desk in a fedora and Gauguin shirt and — *caramba* — it's goodbye to dull old C106 and hello — Copacabana Cocktail Lounge.

I'm really not certain that I . . .

Believe me, Professor Lapping, I do appreciate your anxieties. But then these new campus holidays mean sacrifices all round. I can't imagine that the Chief Librarian is ecstatic about the "Fitness for Over 40's" Jacuzzi in the Accessions Room, or that the Vice Chancellor is exactly over the moon at sharing his office with four senior citizens on the "Get to Know Your Knitting Machine Two-Centre Theme Holiday".

Well, I suppose if everyone has to . . .

That's the spirit. And one other little thing, a possible way you might help us out and not lose touch entirely with your own office during the vacation.

Yes?

Well, I was wondering if by any chance you could possibly play bongos and sing *Una Paloma Blanca* for us on the Deputy Bursar's night off. It would be much appreciated.

And a Proper Sense of Priorities

You in this queue old chap?

Well, yes. I suppose so.

Based in the area?

Of course. We live just over the other side of the . . .

So you'll know that daft bugger Dankers.

I don't think I've had the . . .

Dankworth. Deputy MD regional sales. Balding. Bit of a beer gut. Used to knock off that redhead in systems analysis. Josie something or other.

I think there must be some . . .

You should have seen him last night. You really should. You'd have had to laugh. There we were in the reference library at this O and M shindig. Dankers was well sloshed. Oh yes. Walking round like a mannequin with this great pile of poetry books on his head. Singing *My Way*. What a night!

Very jolly.

Oh yes. Should be a good one tonight as well. Free drinks courtesy of the bursar — whoever he is when he's at home. Disco in that place they call the SCR, and then Croxley's Farewell knees-up in the senate chamber.

Look, you must excuse me. I have to pick up this coffee and then I'm due . . .

NEXT, PLEASE.

Ah yes. Coffee, please. Strongish. You know, dark brown.

Badge?

Pardon?

Are you IBM, sir?

No, of course I'm not. I'm from . . .

Emgas?

What?

108

East Midlands Gas. Because if you are, their coffee's at 10.30. But if you're accountants, it's 10.45.

I don't think you understand. I'm not Emgas or any of the other things. Don't you remember me? I'm a professor. A university professor. *The* pro-**fessor of media and cultural studies. From upstairs. Lapping!**

I'm sorry, dear, but I can't serve you without a badge whatever your name is. It looks like you've made a mistake. Today it's IBM, EMGAS and ACCOUNTANTS. At the weekend, SURVEYORS, CHEMICAL WAR-FARE, and LIBRARIANS. And on Monday and Tuesday, SPASTICS, ESTATE AGENTS, and LOCAL GOVERNMENT. I can't recall anything about PROFESSORS. **Perhaps, you're in the wrong place.**

Conferences Must Be Carefully Concluded

May I first of all say that I think we've had what can only be described as an outstandingly successful conference.

(Cries of "Hear, Hear", and "What about Charlie Odgers falling in the lake on Friday night?")

Well, apart, that is, from Charlie Odgers' unfortunate little experience.

(Loud boorish laughter)

But to speak seriously for a moment. When your committee first decided that the theme for this year's conference should be *Post-Structuralism and Information Technology: Convergences and Prospects,* we expected a large attendance and a great deal of intellectual cut and thrust, and of course, as always a highly enjoyable social occasion. And I think that's exactly what we've all had over the last three days.

So let me straight away offer a most profound vote of thanks to Professor Lapping. I think it's all too easy to take Professor Lapping's work for granted. On the face of it, the job of inviting speakers only involves writing a letter to the eight people selected by the committee. But as anyone who ever tackled this particular task knows only too well, that's only the beginning. There's also the whole business of actually opening the letters of acceptance and reading them. So many thanks to Professor Lapping for all that.

Also, of course, let me as usual, thank Dr. Wernitz and his team of assistants for all the very hard work they did in photocopying the three papers which were made available in advance by the speakers. This is just the sort of backroom work which can so often get overlooked. So, thank you Dr. Wernitz, and perhaps you'd be good enough to convey our thanks in the usual way to your charming assistants.

(Stupid vulgar shout of "Charlie Odgers has done that already". Cackling laughter.)

And, as usual, may I also thank all our speakers. First of all for actually turning up, but also for the prompt way in which they arrived at their own sessions and the general clarity of expression which they brought to the unenviable task of reading out loud from their notes for nearly 30 minutes. Many many thanks to them.

May I also take this opportunity to thank our team of chairmen who have not only been happy to string together a couple of vague phrases at the beginning of each session but have also been ready to call for questions at the end. Thank you gentlemen.

And last but by no means least, may I thank all of you out there.

(Yet another tedious shout of "What about Charlie Odgers?")

Yes, including Charlie Odgers.

(Wholly predictable guffaws of laughter)

I think that we should always remember that without your readiness to give up a weekend of your own time there would be no conference at all. *So,* quite simply, thank *you.*

In conclusion, may I say that we can often forget how difficult it is to remember who to thank and how much to thank them and what one is thanking them for. So, may I, finally, thank myself most sincerely for thanking everyone else.

THANK YOU.

Degrees Sold Overseas

"Academics were accused of using unscrupulous methods in recruiting overseas students at the British Council fair in Kuala Lumpur this week".
— *THES.*

Now, do come a little closer. That's it. Don't block the gangway or we get complaints from the nobs at the British Council. That's it. Now, listen. Have I got some bargains for you today. I tell you, you won't see anything like this on any of the other stalls. Not at twice the price. And remember our guarantee. If you can find a British university degree at a better price than I'm going to sell them for this afternoon — then we'll give you your money back on the spot. No questions asked. And — listen to this — and we'll throw in one of these English Heritage tea towels absolutely *gratis.* Now, you can't say fairer than that, can you?

That's it. Come a little closer. Right, let's make a start. My name's Doctor Wernitz — 'Fair Deal Wernitz' they call me. And I'm going to make a lot of people very very happy this afternoon. And to show that I really do mean business I've got a few oddments here which I'm going to give away for next to nothing — just to get us started. All right?

First of all, would anybody here like a brand new diploma in criminology? This is a one year fully guaranteed diploma which my university is offering to anybody with any sort of undergraduate degree. Forget the subject. Forget the class. Admission to this diploma course is yours at the incredible, knockdown, give-away price of — wait for it — not £5,500, not £5,000, not even £4,500. Here you are. The first six hands I see. Yours for £4,000. That's it. Lady in the second row. Gentleman on the left, and the gentleman behind him. Lady to the right. And the two gentlemen down here at the front. That's your lot. All done. All finished. I tell you, ladies and gentlemen, you need to be on your toes here this afternoon. Oh yes, no hanging about with "Fair Deal Wernitz".

Now then, what have we here? What have we here? Oh yes, look at these beauties. Eight entrance certificates for undergraduate degrees in accountancy. All perfect. No fire damage. You can find the exact same degrees being sold in other parts of this exhibition at this very moment for twice the price. Now one of these could be yours. But remember, we can only serve so many. I've got eight acceptance forms so I don't care if you're the ninth person asking me for one. That's all there is this afternoon.

Now then normally you'd need at least three A levels and 15 grand to get anywhere near one of these magnificent degrees. But I'll tell you what. Forget three A levels. And forget 15 grand. Come on now. There's only these few left. Remember these are fully warranted degrees at one of England's top universities. In six months from now you could be sitting in B and B accommodation in a provincial Midlands town, trying to make yourself understood to a personal tutor, filling in your poll tax identity card and be well on your way to re-sitting a real English degree.

Look, I'll tell you what I'll do. And this is my final offer. Forget those five O levels. Right? Forget those four O levels. Forget three. Here you are, sold to the first six bargain hunters irrespective of qualifications, who can sign a cheque for £12,000. Yes, gentleman on the right, lady on the left . . .

Investments Astutely Managed

Where To Put Your Money. Part IV.

In the wake of the recent stock market shakeout many investors have become less interested in immediate profits and high growth and are instead searching for a safety-first portfolio. This may well make some of the newly privatized universities look rather more attractive than they did pre-slump.

● Having outperformed brokers' expectations at the end of last year, **Leicester University** disappointed many at the half-year stage. Pre-tax profits rose a modest .02 per cent and this sum included £22 profit taking from the sale of disused bikesheds behind the Engineering Tower. Shares fell back further last week with the news that Professor L.T. Shuckworth had decided against taking early retirement.
Verdict: worth watching.

● It's no secret that undergraduate Experimental Theology is a cut-throat business. About half the short-fall in profits this year at **Red Rose University** (formerly, Lancaster) came from losses in this area — with too many places chasing too few students. As a sign of their confidence in **Red Rose's** underlying economy, the Vice Chancellor and the Bursar recently agreed to forgo £15 each of their annual directors' bonus (leaving them with £4.50 each). *Verdict:* **Good value. A one for one scrip is proposed.**

Insert Campus Share Index

● Expect increased profits at **Southampton University** following the arrival from United Biscuits of a new chief executive. Incoming man Ron Spurt has already spoken of the need for a "slimmed-down" workforce and is confidently expected to introduce high-profile low-level degrees along the lines of such previous biscuit successes as "Fudge Fingers" and "Jam Oozies". Despite increased administration costs the development of a tax-efficient offshore fund on the Isle of Wight has helped counter losses arising from a lack of UFC contracts in the labour intensive departments of Macramé and Home Economics.
Verdict: **Well worth a gamble.**

● Applied Phrenology remains **Reading University's** main earner with 4 (four) UFC contracts in this area accounting for 30 per cent of net income. Prospects for future years have also been improved by the success of the Marine Sociology department in repositioning itself up-market with degrees "guaranteed free from Marx".
Verdict: **Solid.**

● Alongside its high reputation in the field of Byzantine Administration, **York University** has strong interests in Creative Accountancy and Panglossian Philosophy, it also holds a picture of the last but one Vice Chancellor which is currently valued at over £20. After two years of sliding profits blamed on unsuccessful diversification into Pre-Thomist Scepticism and Hamburger Retailing (the ill-fated "Heslington Muchburger") **York** may now be set for a period of steady if unsensational growth.
Verdict: **A snip.**

Traditional Ceremonies Re-Assessed

DEGREE DAY

"Pray silence for the Chancellor"
(The deputy bursar lifts the ceremonial mace from stage left and carries it solemnly to the ceremonial table in front of the lectern)
"The Chancellor"
(The Chancellor rises from his place in the centre of the platform party and moves in a slow shuffle to the lectern)
"Vice chancellor, new graduates, honorary graduates, ladies and gentlemen."
(Slow sweeping look around the auditorium)

"I'm certain that you've heard quite enough talking for one morning."
(Slight ripple of amusement among the platform party uncertainly taken up by the audience)
"And you will hardly, therefore, relish another speech from an oldtimer — or in the modern parlance, senior citizen — like myself."
(More restrained amusement)
"So I'm going to be very brief."
(Surveys audience again and gives elaborate hitch to ceremonial garments)
"A very old friend of mine came up to me the other day. Someone I hadn't seen for quite a while. Someone who had just heard of my elevation to your chancellorship."
(Long pause)
"Tell me,' said my friend. 'What on earth is the point of so many of our brightest young people spending three years of their lives at a university when at the end of it all nearly one third of them will be unable to find any sort of work whatsoever?' "
(Some vigorous head-nodding among members of social science faculty)
" 'What on earth is the point?' he repeated. 'Is it because the varied experiences which one is exposed to in a university will stand one in good stead in the monotonous and alienated years which lie ahead?' "
(Signs of platform approval from Professor of Creative English)
" 'Or is it,' he insisted, 'because a university is a training ground for tolerance and self-control and these are the very qualities which will be needed by those who are about to be cast on the scrap heap of life?' "
(Both hands placed on the ceremonial lectern)
" 'Or is it,' demanded my persistent friend, 'or is it because a university is a model of community life which prepares the student for later involvement in such primary groups as the Claimants' Union?' "
(The university orchestra begin to take up instruments in readiness for performance of degree-day hymn: 'With gowns a-flying')
" 'So tell me,' and his voice became quite strident 'exactly what is the point of it all?' "
(Platform party begins to gather bags and ceremonial gowns together)
"Well, I turned to my friend very slowly. Looked him in the eye. And laying one hand gently on his broad shoulder, I said: 'Do you know something, good friend of mine?' "
(Porters move to positions by exit doors)
"I HAVEN'T THE FAINTEST SODDING IDEA."
(Chancellor shuffles back to seat. Platform party rises. Audience stand. Orchestra plays. The ceremony concluded.

Honorary Guests Carefully Selected

Has anyone ever heard of this chap Foucault?
Come again, vice chancellor?
I'm sorry, Professor Stebbing.
FOUCAULT. F-O-U-C-A-U-L-T.
Is he . . . erm . . . French, vice chancellor?
Well, certainly sounds it. *Michel.* That's French for Michael isn't it?
I don't want to be in the slightest nationalistic about this, vice chancellor
. . .

Quite so, Doctor Grampling . . .
But do we really want to hand an honorary degree to some chappie who
may well use the occasion to go blathering on to the assembled parents about
the wonders of existensialism or whatever the current fad is on the Left Bank?
And there is the business of the lambs.
The lambs, Professor Stebbing?
The French, vice chancellor. Burning our lambs.
Oh I see. Yes, yes. Quite so. Well, shall we say "reject list" then?
Definitely
Thank you. May we now move on to the last proposal which is from the
department of English. Melvyn Bragg: writer and broadcaster. Now any
strong views on this nomination? Television chappie.
Isn't he that . . . erm . . . slightly effete fellow?
I don't think he's particularly effete, Professor Ransom.
Is this the chappie who says: "It's nice to see you and nice to see you"?
"Nice to see you: to see you nice", is, I believe, the expression you're after,
Doctor Grampling. No, it's not him, no. But looks like another for the re-
ject list.
Could we now go through the complete reject list, vice chancellor?
Certainly. The full list with our reasons for rejection now reads: Michel
Foucault — too French. E.P. Thompson — too political. Germaine Greer
— too feminist. And Peter Swinnerton-Dyer — too obvious. While our short
list of possible candidates is: Henry Moore, Harold Wilson, Mark Thatcher,
Roy Jenkins and E.F. Sedgecombe.
Thank you, vice chancellor.
Actually, I could perhaps push matters along by declaring a personal
preference for Mr Sedgecombe. Not only is he a local man but he's done
quite excellent work for the inland waterways. He is also a pleasantly modest,
one might almost say, self-effacing man, which I believe fits him well for
such an occasion.
I do so agree with you, vice chancellor. Unfortunately, however, the
strongest evidence for Mr. Sedgecombe's self-effacing charcter also constitutes
an impediment to his present candidature.
In what way, Professor Ransom?
I have just recalled, sir, that we gave him an honorary degree last *year.*

Rituals Choreographed

Ah, vice chancellor. So sorry to barge in without an appointment but I have tried ringing and your secretary always says you're . . .

What is it, Professor Jerger?

Well, sir, it concerns the arrangements for Degree Day.

You're not one of those people who're still bleating about the honorary doctorate for Esther Rantzen?

Not at all, vice chancellor. No, as I made plain in my letter to honorary degrees committeee. I did have a slight preference for Umberto Eco but I quite realize . . .

You're worried about the choice of music for the afternoon?

No, vice chancellor. In fact I've always been a keen admirer of Mr Ellington's symphonic pieces and I'm sure that I shall find *Take the A Train* equally . . . erm . . .

The ceremony then? You're concerned about the ceremony?

Slightly, vice chancellor. Slightly. But let me say straightaway that I have absolutely no objection whatsoever to the arrangements for the *outstanding professors.* There are, I know, one or two of my colleagues who feel that the trumpet fanfare before their entrance is somewhat over-dramatic, but we are all agreed that it is only appropriate that once on stage they should be seated on the golden thrones.

And you're quite happy with the replacement for the traditional hoods?

The crowns with single stars? Oh yes. No complaints there.

Well then, Jerger. Out with it?

Well, sir, I've been asked to say, with what I hope you find is an appropriate humility, that while my department is also quite happy with *above average* and *average professors* standing around the thrones holding silver maces, they do feel a little disturbed that the five *below average professors,* which of course includes myself, should be required to squat cross-legged on the floor and . . .

What on earth's wrong with the floor, Jerger? Perfectly clean.

Nothing at all, vice chancellor. It's not the floor which is creating the mild sense of grievance but the proposed change in ceremonial wear.

But as you know, Jerger, all hoods are being dispensed with this year.

Yes sir, but it's just that members of my department were wondering, in the most respectful way possible, if it was absolutely necessary for their conical replacements to be so evidently inscribed with the large letter "D".

To The Last Detail

TO ALL GRADUANDS
RULES OF PROCEDURE FOR DEGREE DAY 1989

Please make certain that you process to the platform in strict alphabetical order. So, for example, McGreechan always comes before McGreeghan which in turn invariably precedes McGreevey.

All last-minute absences must be immediately reported to the Convener of Degree Day (Wing-Commander D.W.D. Digby). Failure for absences to be noted in the degree lists can result in the unfortunate 'shunting effect' which last year meant that forty-seven graduands were, as they processed across the platform, incorrectly named, and in fourteen cases, erroneously gendered.

Geography graduands are reminded that Professor Collingworth is now in his seventy-third year and therefore not able to sustain a prolonged period of hand-shaking. You are therefore requested to mime this part of the proceedings by placing your hand slightly to the right of his and moving it up and down twice in quick succession.

Graduands may be photographed with a Professor of their choice for the standard fee of £5 per photograph (all proceeds to departmental funds). This offer does not, however, apply this year to Professor Dibson of the Anthropology Department, who is currently of the opinion that repeated exposure to photography has partially robbed him of his identity.

This year's honorary graduates are Mr. J.T.R. Property Developer and Mr. P.B.W. Industrial Effluent. Both men are friends of the university and should be rapturously received both before and after their receipt of the honorary degree. During their lengthy acceptance speeches, laughter should only occur when the presence of a joke is signalled by a thumbs-up from the Deputy Bursar (positioned on the right at the rear of the platform).

We have been advised by Doctor S.Q. Lumiere of the Audio-Visual Unit (the executive producer in charge of this year's degree video) that a higher quality of production will be obtained if the following instructions are at all times observed:

a) All graduands should ensure that their right foot is on 'the chalk mark' when accepting their degrees.

b) A light foundation make-up should be worn at all times

c) On no account must graduands wave in the general direction of the camera when accepting their degree certificates. Rather than guaranteeing a starring role in the video such behaviour will automatically ensure a place on the cutting room floor.

Following a number of representations from individual students, we have decided this year to introduce a special marquee exclusively for those parents who are thought to be 'potentially embarrassing'. Parents who are escorted to this area by their children will not be released until the end of the proceedings.

We are advised by the Vice-Chancellor that, as usual on degree day, he wishes to walk informally among parents and graduates after the ceremony. To avoid a repetition of the unfortunate encounters last year when the vice-chancellor was not recognized by some of those he approached (and indeed on one occasion was the subject of a minor physical assault) we now advise you that he is approximately 5ft 10ins tall, with thinning hair, sallow complexion, and a deep scar running down his right cheek.

Have a nice day.

Even Chancellors Modernized

Wentworth!
Congratulations, Wentworth.
Thank you, sir
Wrigglesworth!
Congratulations, Wrigglesworth.
Thank you, sir
Zukauskas!
Congratulations
Thank you, sir
And two in absentia. And that, my Lord Chancellor concludes the list of the candidates for the award of the bachelor of science degree with honours in zoology. I now call upon the Chancellor of this university to give his annual address.

Vice Chancellor, distinguished guests, academic staff, graduates, parents, step parents, surrogate parents. As usual this year I intend to stand up here and chunter away aimiably about nothing very much for round about three-quarters of an hour after which you will be able to go outside and take some automatic focus pictures of each other before tucking into the very modest helpings of strawberries and single cream laid on by the contracted-out catering services.

As in previous years I will be professing to an intimate knowledge of this university even though, thank God, I never come anywhere near the place except on degree day and even then can hardly make my own way into this crumbling concert hall, let alone on to the makeshift stage without the active assistance of the assistant registrar.

Those of you who follow these events will, however, notice that this year, I am concentrating somewhat less than last year on the central importance to civilization as we know it of such academic values as tolerance, understanding and unfettered intellectual enquiry, and, instead, in acknowledgement of your vice chancellor's carefully considered change of heart over the last twelve months, I will be placing more emphasis on the spiritual enhancement which can be achieved by the enthusiastic espousal of naked greed, crass

materialism, and to hell with the polytechnics.

In conclusion let me say that I myself may not be here to talk to you about such matters next year. As most of you will have gathered from the manner in which I occasionally drop off to sleep, slide from my seat, and talk about the First World War, I am, and indeed always have been, an Old Buffer. We're a proud group. Indeed, it's difficult to imagine how universities might have managed over the years without all those hundreds of Old Buffers who, on graduation days, have shunted slowly backward and forwards across innumerable stages generously conferring honorary degrees on each other. I understand that my place will be taken next year by a prominent manufacturer of condoms — a Young Buffer as one might say *(Pause for laughter)*.

May I then, in conclusion, tidy my notes on the lectern, slowly look up, take off my glasses, stare myopically in your general direction, and mention that a video-cassette of these proceedings is available from the bursar for £18.50. Sorry VHS Only.

Public Admission Of The Need For Change

My Lord Chancellor, Your Grace, Lady Burnt-Chittock, Flight Lieutenant Karamosov, Deputy Superintendent Flaubert, members of Senate and Council, academic staff, parents and of course new graduates of this university. It is my pleasant duty as your Vice Chancellor to use this happy occasion to present my usual brief report on the more interesting changes and developments which have occurred in this university during the last academic year.

As you will know such changes have been principally informed by the need to make economies of just over five million pounds, but it was an essential feature of the original UGC proposals, and, of course, of Sir Keith Joseph's overall strategy for the university sector, that any cuts or economies which might be effected should take the form of a RESTRUCTURING exercise — a significant shift in the fundamental balance of the university.

But let me be a little more specific. Over the year we have reluctantly said "goodbye and good luck in the future" to 145 of our academic colleagues who have taken advantage of the recently introduced early retirement scheme. Some examples will illustrate the principal ways in which these departures have facilitated our aim of restructuring.

In the department of very advanced but highly practical technological studies we find, for example, that a total of 14 staff have selected the early retirement option, and this number includes all three professors together with two readers and four senior lecturers.

Restructuring of a slightly different kind is probably best illustrated by recent developments in the department of steam engineering where all 36 members of staff have decided to maintain their present positions within the university and are busily engaged at the moment in coming to terms with the particular demands created by an 80 per cent reduction in student applications.

I must emphasize that such restructuring is by no means confined to the purely academic level. The department of absolutely essential electronic development has been carefully restructured by the non-replacement of eleven essential technicians, while in the department of vital industrial innovation, restructuring has involved the non-replacement of fourteen academic staff and the continued presence of the previous secretarial staff of five.

Neither should it be thought that the university administration is immune to the type of restructuring which occurs elsewhere on this campus. Non-replacement and early retirement has now ensured the takeover of the bursar's department by the sports centre, and from next month, we look forward to the deputy superintendent (boilerhouse) taking on the additional responsibilities which previously occupied our recently retired registrar.

I think that we can take pride in these last twelve months. There are some who persist in regarding universities as essentially traditional institutions, unable to move with the times, handicapped by adherence to outmoded notions of decision-making.

But what we have seen in the last year is that it is possible for a university community to move with the times — to adapt in the face of economic necessity and ministerial directives. In short, we have seen a wholy commendable readiness to move away from tried and trusted practices, and to abandon ourselves entirely to the operation of *blind chance.*

And Parents Courted

Can I top you up?

Thank you, Professor Lapping.

How did you enjoy all the pomp and circumstance? Glad it's all over?

In a way.

I thought the Chancellor went on a bit. As though there was no tomorrow. Must have thought he was still in the Lords.

Perhaps.

And God knows why they gave an honorary degree to that dreadful old buffoon from the Georgian Society. Talk about death warmed up.

I suppose ...

And the music. How did you like the music?

I'm afraid I'm not all that knowledgeable about classical music, Professor Lapping.

Not into it eh? Not your scene?

Not quite.

No need to apologize. I still enjoy a bit of "pop", you know.

You do?

Oh yes. Only last weekend I was giving a spin to my Tornadoes LP.

Tornadoes?

Yes. You remember. *Telstar. Der der der — Da da dah da da dah.*

I'm afraid not. I'm more interested in Genesis. You know, Phil Collins. And, of course, Elvis.

Say no more. *Yew can dooo anything — but don't yew step on ma blew swede shoos.*

Yes, I have heard that one. But I rather meant Elvis Costello. And The Attractions.

Talking of "attractions". Remember The Swinging Blue Jeans. *For goodness sake — you do the hippy hippy shake.* Oh yes. And Brian Poole and the Trems.

The Trems?

The Tremeloes. Oh yes. Magical stuff. And while we're talking, what about The Honeycombs with that girl drummer. What was her name? *Have I the right to hold you — booom — boom.* Who's your favourite vocalist?

Vocalist? Well, I suppose I particularly enjoy Lou Reed. And Bryan Ferry. And Neil Young — when he's with Crosby, Stills and Nash. And then, probably Jackson Browne.

Jolly good. I like someone who knows what they like and isn't afraid to say so. Well, must circulate a little more. One other thing.

Yes?

If you come across your son before I do, pass on my congratulations on his upper second. We were all delighted. *And keep on grooving!*

I'll do my best.